**America's
Embarrassing Reading Crisis:**

WHAT WE LEARNED FROM COVID

A guide to help educational
leaders, teachers, and parents
change the game

Dr. Lisa Richardson Hassler

America's Embarrassing Reading Crisis:
WHAT WE LEARNED FROM COVID

For more information, contact:
Fig Factor Media, LLC | www.figfactormedia.com

Cover Design by DG Marco Álvarez
Layout by LDG Juan Manuel Serna Rosales

Printed in the United States of America

ISBN: 978-1-957058-40-5
Library of Congress Control Number:

I would like to dedicate this book to my husband, partner in life, and best friend, Gregg Hassler, Jr. He believes that I can do anything and pushes me to be the best version of myself.

ACKNOWLEDGMENTS

I would like to extend my deepest gratitude to those who helped me on my writing journey. This book would not have been possible without the unending support and nurturing from my husband, Dr. Gregg Hassler, Jr. He is my biggest advocate and a constant source of motivation and encouragement. I am humbled by his faith in me.

I would also like to thank my National Louis University dissertation chairs and mentors, Dr. Carla Sparks and Dr. Lorrie Butler. Their collective guidance and support through the dissertation process helped me create work of which I am extremely proud and laid the groundwork for this book. Their consistent communication through weekly check-ins, drop-in Zoom office hours, and timely feedback kept me moving forward. The flexibility, dedication, and passion for education they displayed was inspiring.

Finally, I'm deeply indebted to Eric Robinson. His concern for the reading success of the state's children helped guide me in this direction for further study. He influenced me to use my experience as an elementary teacher and knowledge in online teaching and learning to study an area in education that needed further research. I am forever grateful.

TABLE OF CONTENTS

WELCOME!

I've always loved the feeling of being in the classroom. For over 18 years, I've taught first through fourth grades with the majority of my time in first and second grade. I always wanted to learn more, do more, and incorporate more for my students. So, I kept going back to school, even learning Montessori methods, and blending them into my classroom. My classroom today is a fantastic montage of all the best methods I've learned throughout my years of teaching and learning. It's like the top 100 music hit list of all time. Along my educational journey, I studied reading fluency and virtual school. What I found in my research surprised me and I think will shock you, which is why *I wrote this book.*

That being said, I see the value of face-to-face and distance education. I've taught and been a student in both environments. As an adult, I took classes online and navigated my way through them, but it was a totally different experience than my face-to-face college classes. It took much more discipline.

Later, I earned a master's degree in online teaching and learning. It was future minded I thought at the time. How would I have known what was to come? I, like many, saw the world struggle in 2020 with the coronavirus pandemic and experienced the impact as our brick-and-mortar school doors closed and virtual school doors opened. I switched from teaching my face-to-face second-grade students to teaching online. The following year, I taught second grade concurrently with half of my class face-to-face and the other half online. My background and training gave me the foundation to survive such turmoil. Still, I saw how this affected teachers and students in my school. The experience made me realize that virtual education is more than a charter school option; it is an educational reality that affects all teachers, students, and families.

Before you start this book, you need to know a few things to make the most of your time. First, virtual school, online education, e-learning, and distance education are interchangeable terms. Many studies use these terms with the same overall meaning as a program created for student education using an Internet technology platform with a teacher.

Second, there are two parts. Part 1, Virtual School and Reading Success, highlights the current national reading problem. This lays the foundation for the need for urgent change. Chapter 2 takes a plunge into virtual school, its history and track record with documented success. Part 1 ends with comparing face-to-face and virtual school reading success in third grade. The data here will surprise you and should be used as the base for building change in education.

Part 2 is a guide to improve the modern classroom from three major stakeholders in education: educational decision makers, teachers, and parents. Chapter 4 shows how virtual education can be used in our brick-and-mortar schools and in our homes using what we learned from the coronavirus pandemic.

Then, the following three chapters are reader driven. Educational leaders will want to flip to Chapter 5, Envisioning Change, for a guide to make policy changes to increase teacher and student success for their states and school districts. Teachers can go right to Chapter 6, Envisioning Success, to guide their instruction and platform creating for the best student achievement outcome. Parents will want to go straight to Chapter 7, Envisioning Control, to increase reading fluency and navigate online learning for you and your child.

Finally, I end this book with Lead to Shape and Inspire, leaving a path to make change. Through the process of writing my dissertation and writing this book, I have grown as a leader in my ability to use scholarly research to investigate a problem in my field and community to create change. I learned about the power of politics in the field of education and realized the impact school district leaders have as they create policies. From this process, I created 4 steps on how you, the stakeholder, can be part of the process to create change for better communities and schools. Teachers, parents, and policy makers need to know the validity of online learning when implemented with theory and how to use it to increase literacy. Overall, just focus on the children and their success. It really is just that simple.

Part 1

Virtual School
and
Reading Success

Chapter 1:

THE READING PROBLEM

Forty-four percent of third graders in Florida are not reading proficiently. Twenty-one percent of those third graders are at risk for failing. These numbers are embarrassing and are only getting worse.

There is a major concern for third grade reading proficiency and The Department of Education and politicians say that they are going to improve it. It's a big deal if you're a teacher or parent. No one likes to fail, and it doesn't look so good right now, but *Florida is not alone.* Turns out the whole country is looking at numbers like this.

CRITICAL ACADEMIC INDICATORS

So, why third grade? Why isolate that grade level? As it turns out, reading on grade level in third grade matters quite a lot.

Third grade reading proficiency is linked with student success later in life, both academically and economically. In a Kids Count special report by the Annie E. Casey Foundation, author Leila Fiester stated, "Reading proficiency by the end of third grade (as measured by National Assessment of Educational Progress at the beginning of fourth grade) can be a make-or-break benchmark in a child's development."[1] She also said, "Three-quarters of students who are poor readers in third grade will remain poor readers in high school." The National Center for Education Statistics (1995), as reported by Snow et al., stated:

> Academic success, as defined by high school graduation, can be predicted with reasonable accuracy by knowing someone's reading skills at the end of third grade... A person who is not at least a modestly skilled reader by that time is unlikely to graduate high school.[2]

Fiester linked high school graduation and future student success when she stated, "Low achievement in reading has important long-term consequences in terms of individual earning potential, global competitiveness, and general productivity."[3] High school dropouts have an earning potential of half of what a student who completed a bachelor's degree or higher would earn, directly impacting their economic self-sufficiency.

Leila Fiester later wrote a follow-up report for the Annie E. Casey Foundation in 2013, *Early Warning Confirmed:*

[1] L. Fiester (2010). *Early warning! Why reading by the end of third grade matters.* In Annie E. Casey Foundation (pp. 1–62). https://www.aecf.org/resources/earlywarning-why-reading-by-the-end-of-third-grade-matters/

[2] C. Snow, Burns, S., & Griffin, P. (1998). - National Academy Press. https://files.eric.ed.gov/fulltext/ED416465.pdf

[3] L. Fiester (2010). *Early warning! Why reading by the end of third grade matters.* In Annie E. Casey Foundation (pp. 1–62). https://www.aecf.org/resources/earlywarning-why-reading-by-the-end-of-third-grade-matters/

A Research Update on Third-Grade Reading, to revisit the 2010 findings. The Kids Count special report confirmed that the academic gap between fluent and struggling readers did not diminish over time.[4] In one study, Canadian researchers, McNamara et al., conducted a longitudinal study of 382 kindergarten children and found that students with low reading proficiency were likely to remain low from kindergarten through Grade 3.[5] Additionally, the reading gap increased as children continued in school, with struggling readers falling further behind in grade-level reading than their peers. Donald J. Hernandez's study of over 4,000 students corroborated Fiester's 2010 report confirming critical indicators. Hernandez reported that "children who do not read proficiently by the end of third grade are four times more likely to leave school without a diploma than proficient readers."[6]

In 2014, Hanover Research reported additional findings in Critical Academic Indicators research on the importance of reading proficiency in third grade. Hernandez confirmed the relationship between third grade reading proficiency and high school graduation using a sample of 3,975 students born between 1979 and 1989. He tracked the sample students' reading progress every two years using a reading recognition subtest of the Peabody Individual Achievement Test (PIAT). Of the student sampling, 16% of students not

---

[4] L. Fiester (2013). *Early warning confirmed.* In Annie E. Casey Foundation (pp. 1–29), Annie E. Casey. http://grade-levelreading.net/wpcontent/uploads/2013/11/EarlyWarningConfirmed.pdf

[5] McNamara et al., 2011, as cited in Fiester, 2013

[6] D. J. Hernandez (2012). *Double jeopardy: How third-grade reading skills and poverty influence high school graduation.* The Annie E. Casey Foundation.

reading proficiently in third grade failed to graduate by age 19. Hernandez stated that one in six children not reading proficiently in third grade fail to graduate high school on time which is four times the rate for children who did read proficiently in third grade. Additionally, third grade reading proficiency was identified as one of the "On-Track Indicators" by The Community Center for Education Results (2013) for students to be on track to earn a college degree or career credential.[7] Third grade reading proficiency matters.

Jen Elise Prescott et al. remarked on the importance of acting on the critical academic indicator in the article, *Elementary School-Wide Implementation of a Blended Learning Program for Reading Intervention.*[8] She supported Fiester's views on the importance of being a proficient reader by Grade 3. It is a key predictor of future academic and career success. She went on to state, "Thus, there is an urgent need to identify instructional approaches that can effectively boost reading skills in elementary school students, particularly those from low-SES [socioeconomic status] backgrounds and students who are ELs [English Learners]." In summary, if identified reading instructional practices are used to increase reading fluency in struggling readers by Grade 3, their future academic and career success will also increase.

The indicators continue. There is a link between students

---

[7] The Community Center for Education Results. (2013). *The Road Map Project 2013 results report.* The Community Center for Education Results.
https://roadmapproject.org/wp-content/uploads/2018/09/2013-Results-Report_Reduced-File-Sz.pdf
[8] J. E. Prescott, Bundschuh, K., Kazakoff, E. R., & Macaruso, P. (2018). Elementary school-wide implementation of a blended learning program for reading intervention.

who do not read on grade level and incarceration. According to ExcelinEd, an education reform group, "More than 80 percent of students who fail to earn a high school diploma were struggling readers in third grade." After high school dropout, the student's outlook gets very bleak.

- Almost 85 percent of teenagers in the juvenile justice system are functionally illiterate.
- Seven out of 10 adult prisoners can't read above a fourth-grade level.
- Dropouts make up 90 percent of Americans on welfare and 75 percent of food stamp recipients.

Figure 1

Third Grade Indicators with Possible Results

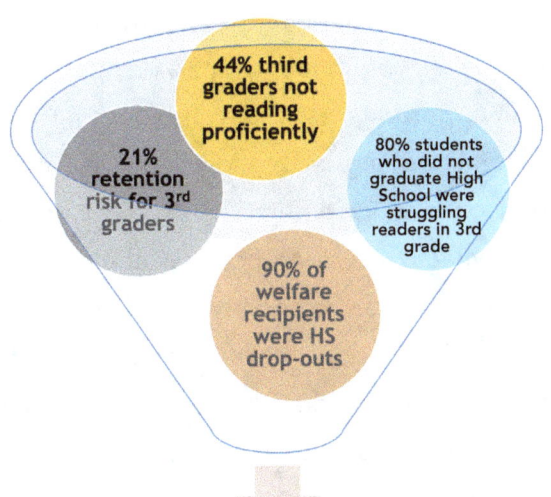

Seven out of 10 adult prisoners can't read above a fourth-grade level.

The best thing a state or local education decision maker, educator, and parent can do for a child is have children read on grade level in third grade. There is no magic make up year that can ever close the academic gap at that point. Struggling readers will remain behind compared to their classmates. No child should end up with the future these indicators foretell. Something must change. Society needs to be open to that change because any improvement saves children's future lives.

TESTING FOR READING DISABILITY

It's scary when you think of the connection reading on grade level in third grade has as a predictor on a child's future success and the impact it has on society. While it sounds dramatic, teachers do know the students that struggle academically year after year. Early screening at the kindergarten level combined with early intervention can help. The three most interested stakeholders in this process are parents, teachers, and educational leaders. They are the three spokes to the child centered wheel. If they could agree on when and what to test for to increase reading proficiency, then progress could start rolling towards a better future.

Children usually take high stakes assessments at the state level starting in third grade. The learning foundation for that test, however, starts long before that, in pre-school and kindergarten. So, what kind of assessments are they taking to monitor reading progress and what is being done with that information?

Currently, Florida requires statewide kindergarten readiness testing for all public school students within the first 30 days of school and for the Voluntary Prekindergarten (VPK) Education Program. Nonpublic schools may administer Florida Kindergarten Readiness Screener (FLKRS) using Renaissance Star Early Literacy test, to each kindergarten student who was previously enrolled in VPK. The results measure early literacy skills of beginning readers directly related to their future reading success.

What happens when a child does not meet a benchmark? The educational system gets complicated here. *Here's a Typical Example as to How the System Fails:*

Usually what happens is that parents are notified, teachers provide tiered interventions, and everything is documented. The kindergarten year can easily pass by waiting. There is waiting for students to mature if they had birthdays close to the cutoff date and waiting for those students who did not attend preschool to catch up to their peers who did. The teacher and parents seem to hold their breath and wait for the internal click within the struggling child to turn on and "get it." Recommendations are given. Summer comes and goes.

Now, the student enters first grade; a new year, a new teacher, and new hopes. At this point, reading running records are done with students to record their fluency. When fluency benchmarks are not met, parents are again notified. Teachers increase tiered interventions for those students who didn't meet the milestones again and everything is documented. Data collection is continued and is used to request further testing to find out why the student is struggling. This is an ideal time to test for a reading disability. Another summer comes and goes.

The student then enters second grade. More running records are done, parents are notified again, teachers increase tiered interventions once more. Another year can easily slip by without reading disability identification and intense reading interventions. Meanwhile the optimal time for effective interventions has diminished.

The student is now in third grade. Learning changes. Students are expected to read on grade level to comprehend the subject material and read to learn, not learn to read. The optimum time to diagnose a reading disability and implement intense interventions has passed. At this point and here after, it's much harder for the brain and the gains are smaller.

What's broken here is not the recording process of missed milestones, or tiered interventions, that's solid. It's the process of testing to discover *the reason* a student is not reaching benchmarks. So much time goes by documenting outcomes of tiered interventions during the primary grade, that learning disabilities are not caught in time. If learning disabilities were caught in kindergarten and first grade, interventions geared towards that disability could have been used for intense interventions increasing the child's chances to read on grade level. It is proven that students that were low in kindergarten, continue to be low in first, second, and third grade. It is also proven that after second grade, interventions for reading are less effective. The academic gap continues to widen over the student's academic career at that point. They never catch up with their peers.

So why are student disabilities not being identified through testing earlier? That's where parents and policy get introduced. More often than you'd think, parents do not believe the teacher that their child is struggling. Many parents do not pursue the recommended testing based on the response to intervention for their child. Oftentimes, parents feel attacked and angry, become defensive of their child, and redirect focus onto the teacher's abilities. All the while waiting for the next school year, hoping the next teacher is going to be the difference.

When parents do partner with the teacher, they are often set for a battle against policy. The amount of documentation and time it takes to get a child tested for a disability through the educational system is frustrating and wastes valuable time. Each intervention needs to be implemented and documented for six weeks before a meeting takes place to discuss the results and suggest another intervention. Years of school can pass like this. It's more efficient to get a child tested through private channels, but not everyone knows where to go, how to navigate it, or has the money to pay. It can be an extremely daunting task.

Once the recommended physician tests are complete, meetings are set up and formal documentation is set in place giving the students the services they need, but not always. Private schools do not have to follow these plans. How is this allowed? If a school accepts a child, then they should be required to provide all services for their education. If the school cannot meet the plan's expectations, then the child should go to a school that does. There should not be an exception to this. Remember the goal is to help children reach their maximum academic potential. Keeping students at schools that cannot provide for them only hurts them.

If educational leaders and policy makers really wanted to fix the reading problem, they would. They know the academic indicators. They know what they mean. There's not an urban myth about prisons planning their future beds based on third grade reading levels for no reason.

Yet, the red tape and optional testing continue. Parents do not know this information. I guarantee it. No child comes with a manual that tells them this. Teachers are not allowed to speak directly about this to parents. They can only request the parent take their child to their pediatrician for further evaluation.

So, the parents drive the bus blindfolded and full of children. Teachers stand on the curb watching in horror, duct tape over their mouths. The policy makers and educational leaders build a sleek new road and buy a fancy new bus. The bus crashes. Come on, we knew it would. It's time to take the blindfolds off parents.

Policy makers need to support disability testing by making it easier to access when early red flags are raised for reading benchmarks not met by students. Speed up the process. Every day matters. Enforce that all student support plans be strictly followed, regardless of the school they attend. Fund services needed to support these academic plans. It costs families and communities more to deal with poverty and prison than early identification and intervention.

Chapter 2:

VIRTUAL SCHOOL: A DEEPER DIVE

K-2 education has changed as more parents choose online education for their children. According to the department of education, virtual education has gained acceptance and popularity as a charter school option. However, the coronavirus pandemic in 2020-2021, took that choice away from families and forced most brick-and-mortar schools in the United States to switch from face-to-face environments to online platforms. Virtual School became more than a charter school option. It is an educational reality that affects all students. With no options left, teachers and students were forced into a virtual reality few had prepared for.

HISTORY

The available literature on virtual school student success is focused on the main educational areas of elementary school, high school, and undergraduate school. There are more studies on undergraduate student success because it has been established the longest. Distance education premiered in adult course work as mail correspondence in 1840 in England, expanded into broadcasting television through the British Open University in 1969, and became web-based emerging onto the university scene worldwide in 1995.[9] Since 1996, K-12 online education has become "a major phenomenon" in the United States, and many school districts face competition from homeschooling, charter schools, and private schools starting virtual schools. Florida jumped on the virtual school scene and started the United States' first statewide virtual school, Florida Virtual School (FLVS), in 1997.[10] Florida then implemented a state-wide requirement in 2012 that high school students must complete one online course for high school graduation with a 24-credit standard diploma. With more students required to take virtual classes, data on high school students increased.

[9] J. M. Spector, Merrill, M. D., van Merrienboer, J., Driscoll, M. P., Hannafin, R. D., & Young, M. F. (2014). *Handbook of research on educational communications and technology.* Springer.

[10] J. Hughes, Zhou, C., Petscher, Y., Regional Educational Laboratory Southeast (ED), & Florida State University, F. C. for R. R. (2015). Comparing success rates for general and credit recovery courses online and face to face: results for Florida high school courses. REL 2015-095. *In Regional Educational Laboratory Southeast.*

One such virtual school in the United States in Florida Virtual School, or FLVS as it is commonly referred to. FLVS was established in 1997 as a grant-based pilot project, pioneering the state's first Internet-based, public high school. In 2021, as a fully accredited, statewide public-school district, FLVS offered more than 190 online courses to students in Kindergarten-Grade 12. Certified teachers used a variety of personalized instructional programs to create individualized educational plans for students.

Since 1997, FLVS students have completed more than 4.6 million semester enrollments. FLVS also provided its courseware to online and blended learning programs across the nation. Students attending FLVS were also required to take the state assessments for third grade, so there was viable comparable data on third-grade student achievement in the area of English Language Arts. As a not-for-profit, FLVS reinvested funds into developing new educational technologies and creating courses for students in the state and globally.

Despite recommendations from authors of various articles and reports like Patrick and Powell in 2009, there had been no large-scale studies across a state comparing online and traditional students in the primary grades using state achievement data until 2021. The current nation-wide problem with low achieving third graders and the need to know more about the success of online education at this grade level, made a study in this area necessary to make informed judgements by state and local education decision makers.

ELEMENTARY ONLINE EDUCATION STUDIES

There was a gap in the literature with rigorous studies on student achievement for second-grade students in online schools. Many studies grouped K-12 generically to then focus on a specific area outside of second grade. With that in mind, there were also no rigorous studies on any primary grades (kindergarten through second grade) for student success in online schools.[11] The studies discussed in the elementary (kindergarten through grade eight) online education section ranged from e-learning environments to blended classrooms, to virtual schools.

In the article, *The Effectiveness of E-Learning Environment in Developing Academic Achievement and the Attitude to Learn English Among Primary Students,* Dr. Afaf M. Aljaser identified the effectiveness of the e-learning environment in developing academic achievement along with increased attitudes in learning English with fifth-grade students.[12] E-learning in this study was defined as a real environment with electronic tools. Aljaser designed an online learning environment English class according to the Analyze, Design, Develop, Implement, Evaluate (ADDIE) educational design model to test how e-learning could be used to improve student achievement in and attitude towards learning English. Students were given pre- and post-

---

[11] Molnar, Miron, G., Elgeberi, N., Barbour, M. K., Huerta, L., Shafer, S. R., & Rice, J.K. (2019). *Virtual schools in the US 2019.* National Education Policy Center; NEPC. https://nepc.colorado.edu/publication/virtual-schools-annual-2019

[12] A. M. Aljaser (2019). The effectiveness of e-learning environment in developing academic achievement and the attitude to learn English among primary students. *Turkish Online Journal of Distance Education* (TOJDE), 20(2), 176–194.

teaching achievement tests and English learning attitude scales to measure academic growth and attitude. Aljaser used a control group of 15 randomly selected students using the brick-and-mortar traditional method and an experimental group of 15 randomly selected students using the e-learning environment in Saudi Arabia. The e-learning environment combined synchronous and asynchronous communication tools, a high structure of course design, and learner interests. He found that learners in the experimental group felt engaged and motivated by the online learning environment with a higher degree of dialogue and timely feedback, aligning with the Theory of Transactional Distance by Dr. Michael G. Moore. Additionally, the e-learning classroom had higher achievement scores in both the post achievement test and the English learning attitude scale. While this study was not based upon a fully online course, it showed how dialogue, structure, and learner autonomy could impact student success in distance education.

Jen Elise Prescott et al. described their study in the article, *Elementary School-Wide Implementation of a Blended Learning Program for Reading Intervention,* on kindergarten through Grade 5 student success in a blended environment for literacy instruction. Prescott et al. defined blended learning as having face-to-face components and teacher-led instruction while optimizing digital technology to enhance differentiated instruction. They used this blended learning model to study the effects blended learning would have on student achievement because there "is an urgent need to identify instructional approaches that can effectively boost reading skills in elementary school students."[13]

The study by Prescott et al. included 722 participants representing kindergarten through Grade 5 students in 31 classrooms from October through May of the 2014-2015 school year. After a whole-school implementation of Core5, the blended learning program, results showed overall gains in reading skills, particularly in comprehension. Overall, the most significant growth was in kindergarten, first, and second grade, respectively. Growth was minimal in Grades 3-5. This was interesting because it showed that introducing an online component to a language arts program can increase student achievement but that it diminished to small gains after second grade.

Sherrill Waddell studied the effectiveness of virtual school size and its impact on student achievement in her study, *Examining the Relationship Between Virtual School Size and Student Achievement.*[14] The achievement was measured by the State of Texas Assessments of Academic Readiness (STAAR) in the areas of English Language Arts/ Reading and Math for Grades 5 and 8, and English 1, English 11, and Algebra 1 for Grades 9-12. Data was analyzed from the state education website for all fifth-grade virtual school students and eighth through twelfth-grade virtual school

[13] J. E. Prescott, Bundschuh, K., Kazakoff, E. R., & Macaruso, P. (2018). Elementary school-wide implementation of a blended learning program for reading intervention. *Journal of Educational Research, 111*(4), 497–506. https://doi-org.nl.idm.oclc.org/10.1080/00220671.2017.1302914

[14] S. Waddell (2017). Examining the relationship between virtual school size and student achievement. Quarterly Review of Distance Education, 18(4), 23–35.

students in Texas for the years 2013-2016 for a total of 6,477 participants. She found that "In general, the students in the smaller schools performed significantly better across the three school years." Additionally, "in all testing categories, students performed better in small virtual schools than large virtual schools in all racial categories." Waddell advocated for virtual school as a cost-effective way to educate students.

Gulnara M. Burdina et al. wrote the article, *Distance Learning in Elementary School Classrooms: An Emerging Framework for Contemporary Practice* and conducted a study with 430 online school students aged 8-9 years old in 29 schools in Kazan, Republic of Tatarstan (Russia).[15] Burdina et al. found that students need socialization and a teacher mentor to raise academic performance and motivation. They compared the students' progress through surveys and course grades twice. First, they surveyed and analyzed grade data in the existing course structure and found that 11% of students received As, 23% received Bs, 40% received Cs, 17% received Ds, and 9% received Es. Burdina et al. then made a change in the online courses' structure to allow for increased dialogue of student-student and student-teacher in the form of no structure chat rooms and low structure teacher mentoring. The change in course structure made a significant improvement in student achievement and motivation. At the end of the course, 26% of students received As, 39% received Bs, 27% received Cs, 8% received

---

[15] G. M. Burdina, Krapotkina, I. E., & Nasyrova, L. G. (2019). Distance learning in elementary school classrooms: An emerging framework for contemporary practice. *International Journal of Instruction*, 12(1), 1–16.

Ds, and 0% received Es. This study showed high dialogue and course structure impact on student achievement in a virtual school learning environment.

HIGH SCHOOL ONLINE STUDIES

In a study questioning which factors affect student achievement in a K-12 online school, researchers Heidi Curtis and Loredana Werth focused on one online high school in the Western United States. The article is *Fostering Student Success and Engagement in a K-12 Online School.*[16] Eight parents of online students were selected to participate in semi-structured, one-on-one interviews. Each participant was interviewed twice.

The authors of the study had several findings. First, parents of self-motivated, fully engaged, and accountable students found online school to be pleasant and rewarding. Second, parents of students unsuccessful in online schooling had been unsuccessful in multiple school settings. Third, parents were looking for an individualized student learning experience. The flexibility and control those students had online was helpful and motivated students to learn in some instances. Still, in other cases, freedom increased student failure. Fourth, communication should be to both parents and students. Fifth, parents wanted better communication on available resources to engage in school more effectively and avoid student failure. Sixth, the online classes'

---

[16] H. Curtis, & Werth, L. (2015). Fostering student success and engagement in a K-12 online school. *Journal of Online Learning Research, 1*(2), 163–190.

transparency through the Learning Management System (LMS) was appreciated by the parents and gave them the knowledge they needed to assist their children. Overall, Curtis and Werth found that "No single factor affects student achievement in a full-time high school. Participants' shared perceptions demonstrated that students' achievement is affected by the performance of the school, students, and parents."

Susan R. McNally analyzed the effectiveness of online schools for part-time students in grades 6-12 in the state of Florida. Students were seeking to fulfill graduations requirements or increase a D or F for GPA improvement. In her study, *The Effectiveness of Florida Virtual School in Terms of Cost and Student Achievement in a Selected Florida Virtual School District*, McNally discussed the importance of engagement to increase student success like Curtis and Werth did. McNally stated, "Time and time again, students indicated they were successful in online courses because of the interaction they had with their teacher, and that they received more individualized and focused instruction in an online course."[17] She found that there was an 18%-43% withdrawal rate with students over the three years of the study. Additionally, "students enrolled in the FLVS courses earned considerably more failing grades in the courses." McNally stated:

---

[17] S. R. McNally (2012). *The effectiveness of Florida virtual school in terms of cost and student achievement in a selected Florida school district* [Doctoral dissertation, University of Florida]. ProQuest LLC.

In light of the high percentage of withdrawals from each course, coupled with the high percentage of failures in the three courses, the use of FLVS for these particular courses did not support academic achievement or student success during the three years of the study, based solely on this particular analysis.

However, in a study by the non-profit taxpayer research institute and watchdog group, Florida Tax Watch, student achievement in middle and high school students were found to be a credible alternative to traditional schools. FLVS was given "high marks" in the report.[18]

UNDERGRADUATE ONLINE STUDIES

Manya Suresh et al. conducted a questionnaire-based study in 2018, *Effect of E-Learning on the Academic Performance of Undergraduate Students*.[19] For this study, e-learning was defined as a course taken online. Sixty-one participants between the ages of 18 and 21 took a 14-question online survey based on learning aids used, understanding capacity, and feasibility. Sixty-seven percent of participants preferred interactive e-learning. Forty-one percent of participants claimed to have understood the course subject fully. Seventy-five percent of participants stated that they found e-learning courses made learning

[18] Florida Tax Watch. (2007). *Final report: A comprehensive assessment of Florida Virtual School.* https://floridataxwatch.org/Research/Full-Library/ArtMID/34407/ArticleID/16048/Final-Report-A-Comprehensive-Assessment-of-Florida-Virtual-School

[19] M. Suresh, Vishnu Priya, V., & Gayathri, R. (2018). Effect of e-learning on academic performance of undergraduate students. *Drug Invention Today, 10*(9), 1797–1800.

faster and deeper. In contrast, the remaining 25% of participants felt that e-learning took more time and was harder. Thirty-eight percent of participants stated that e-learning improved their academic performance. Suresh et al. concluded that "e-learning helps to improve the academic performance of undergraduate students."

Thomas Chatman et al. found that online education "requires a different skill set compared to traditional face-to-face instruction" in the study, *Increasing Success with Online Degree Courses and Programs in the VCCS*. Chatman et al. gathered data from the Virginia Community College System (VCCS) from 2015-2016, 2016- 2017, and 2017-2018.[20] They found that out of 724,116 online classes taken by students, in 206,533 of the classes students either withdrew or failed (grade D or F), making a total of 29% of unsuccessful student completions of online courses. This percentage did not include students who dropped the course early in the semester.

To discover why there was such a high rate of failure in online courses from this data, Chatman et al. conducted a small focus group discussion with students taking online courses in VCCS. They found that two major factors contributed to the high failure rate: student preparedness and accessibility. Students did not have the self-regulatory skills necessary and were unfamiliar with the online learning management system. Additionally, 12% of students did not

[20] T. Chatman, Dick, D., Ford, P., Henry, P., Hobert, K., Keller, M., Riley, K., Tidwell, C., & Wright, R. (2019). Increasing success with online degree courses and programs in the VCCS. *Inquiry, 22*(1), 1-15.

have Internet access. Chatman et al. suggested creating a mandatory online orientation for all new online students and working with the community to provide Internet access in homes for students without Internet access. An online orientation would increase the successful completion of online courses.

In the study, *A Case Study Comparing Students Experiences and Success in an Undergraduate Mathematics Course Offered Through Online, Blended, and Face-to-Face Instruction,* by Virginia L. Thompson and Yonghong L. Mc Dowell, the authors gathered data from students in three types of learning environments to analyze.[21] Thompson and McDowell concluded that "students can attain the same level of academic achievement through online, blended, and face-to-face courses (measured through final exam and course final grades)." Ninety-five participants took the same mathematics course, Computer Algebra Systems (CAS), grouped into online, blended, and face-to-face classes. Most online and blended learning students had a satisfactory experience when surveyed, with the area of most concern being working in groups online. Thompson and McDowell stated that "students can achieve equal academic success across online, blended, and face-to-face courses."

Mark Brown et al. conducted a study in Australia to capture the motivation and experiences of college students in online courses. Twenty first-time online learners created weekly video

---

[21] V. L. Thompson, & McDowell, Y. L. (2019). A case study comparing student experiences and success in an undergraduate mathematics course offered through online, blended, and face-to-face instruction. *International Journal of Education in Mathematics, Science and Technology, 7*(2), 116–136.

diaries in response to a reflective prompt from the researchers during their first semester. Brown et al. concluded:

> The new digital learning environment made possible by the Internet offers a number of exciting possibilities for distance learners; however, more needs to be done by institutions to change the "lone wolf" preconception of distance education and to avoid the "goulash approach" to supporting distance learners.[22]

Students have "relatively little concept of what it is like to study by distance," and that creates a high-risk transition period during the first six weeks of an online course. Brown et al. also found that there were many "shades of grey" like family support and responsibilities, job responsibilities, health, and home environment as well as academic preparedness and student attributes, that also contributed to online learners' success that was behind the high amount of course failure.

THEORY

Virtual learning, online learning, distance education, whatever you call it, is not a new concept. Michael G. Moore first attempted to articulate a theory to define distance education in 1972.[23] In this original theory, he stated:

[22] M. Brown, Hughes, H., Keppell, M., Hard, N., & Smith, L. (2015). Stories from students in their first semester of distance learning. *International Review of Research in Open & Distance Learning, 16*(4), 1–17. https://doiorg.nl.idm.oclc.org/10.19173/irrodl.v16i4.1647

[23] M. Moore (1997). *Theory of transactional distance.* In D. Keegan (Ed.), Theoretical principles of distance education (pp. 22–38). Routledge.

Distance education is not simply a geographic separation of learners and teachers, but more importantly, is a pedagogical concept. It is a concept describing the universe of teacher-learner relationships that exist when learners and instructors are separated by space and/or time.

Moore then expanded on his original theory and described transactional distance (TD) as the psychological and communications space that occurs between teachers and learners with the special characteristic of separation. TD profoundly affects teachers and learners and leads to "special patterns of learner and teacher behaviors." Moore broke TD into three areas, referred to as clusters. The first two clusters describe teaching procedures in Dialogue and Structure. The third cluster, Learner Autonomy, describes learner behaviors.

Instructional Dialogue is developed by teachers and learners in a purposeful, constructive way that improves student understanding in the educational relationship. Moore stated that the teachers and learners in a dialogue needed to be respectful and active listeners by contributing and building on the contributions of each party involved. Distance education was just beginning at the time Moore was developing his theory. He made this statement for the future:

As the distance of education field matures, it is to be hoped that greater attention will be paid to variables besides the communication media, especially the design of courses and the selection and training of instructors, and the learning style of students.

Program Structure consists of variables that determine TD through course design.The flexibility and rigidity of a course's educational objectives, evaluation methods, and teaching strategies describe to what extent they can meet each learner's individual needs. Moore described the different effects on TD through program design in his statement:

When a programme is highly structured, and teacher learner dialogue is nonexistent, the transaction between learners and teachers is high. At the other extreme, there is low transactional distance in those teleconference programmes that have much dialogue and little predetermined structure.

Moore recommended six processes to be structured in every distant educational course. The first is the presentation in which he encouraged recorded media as the most powerful when presenting new information, modeling, or demonstrating a skill. The second is the *support of the learner's motivation*. Learner support is accomplished through stimulating the course content to be of the student's interest, stimulation through film, feedback, and unstructured teacher-learner dialogue. The third is to *stimulate analysis and criticism* with associated attitudes and values through teleconference with a recorded or printed presentation or recorded media.

The fourth process is to *give advice and counsel.* The course must guide how to use the learning materials, study techniques, and references for help to develop study skills and help with study problems. Guidance can be done electronically through the course shell or individual dialogue. The fifth is to *arrange practice, application, testing, and evaluation.* Students must be allowed to apply what they are learning, practice skills, and manipulate information. Even self-directed learners are vulnerable at the application process. The opportunity for dialogue is essential to assist the student in testing and getting feedback. Finally, the sixth process is to *arrange for student creation of knowledge.* Students need to have the opportunity for meaningful dialogue with teachers to create knowledge.

The third and final cluster is Learner Autonomy. Moore described this as "the extent to which in the teaching/ learning relationship it is the learner rather than the teacher who determines the goals, the experiences, and the evaluation decisions of the learning program." After analysis of the data, Moore recognized personality characteristic patterns among students who preferred and succeeded in highly dialogic and less structured programs and those who preferred and succeeded in less dialogic and more structured programs. He suggested that teachers assist students; in this case, they were adult learners, acquiring the skills for self-directed learning.

Overall, Moore was excited about the personal computer and its usefulness in distance education as having enormously significant implications in teaching-learning. He described the engagement of collective intelligence, virtual groups, and students' individuality to interact in their own time and pace. Moore's Theory of Transactional Distance is still relevant today, especially in advancements in technology commonly used in distance education to reduce TD and improve student achievement.

In 2015, Huang et al. researched Moore's Theory of Transactional Distance, as documented in the study, *Measuring Transactional Distance in Web-Based Learning Environments: An Initial Instrument Development.*[24] Huang et al. developed and validated a measuring instrument for TD. Data from 227 online students suggested that the instrument could be used to measure TD for online courses. This measuring instrument proved useful for improving future online course design and instruction methods to bridge the "psychological and communications space."

Xiaoxia Huang et al. continued to research Moore's theory of TD in their study, *Understanding Transactional Distance in*

---

[24] X. Huang, Chandra, A., DePaolo, C., Cribbs, J., & Simmons, L. (2015). Measuring transactional distance in web-based learning environments: an initial instrument development. *Open Learning, 30*(2), 106–126

Web-Based Learning Environments: An Empirical Study, and were able to provide evidence to support Moore's Theory of Transactional Distance (TD) as applicable to current online learning environments with newer types of instructional media and changing learner demographic attributes.[25] Huang et al. addressed the impacts of the three constructs of dialogue, structure, and learner autonomy in TD. The researchers found that high dialogue (+D) and high structure (+S) led to the least perceived TD. In contrast, low dialogue (-D) and low structure (-S) led to the highest TD, and in between were high dialogue and low structure (+D-S) and low dialogue and high structure (-D+S). Huang et al. suggested that online instructors use +D+S, synchronous communication tools, and require student discussions to reduce TD. Huang et al. warned that special attention needed to go to the students required to take online courses but preferred face-to-face courses. The research of Huang et al. also found that the older the students (aged 25 and older), the more autonomous they were compared to younger students (aged 18-24).

[25] X. Huang, Chandra, A., DePaolo, C. A., & Simmons, L. L. (2016). Understanding transactional distance in web-based learning environments: An empirical study. *British Journal of Educational Technology,* 47(4), 734–747.https://doi.org/10.1111/bjet.12263

Chapter 3:

FACE TO FACE AND VIRTUAL SCHOOL: HOW DO THEY COMPARE?

Face to Face Instruction

Virtual Instruction

So how does the success of students in traditional classrooms compare to that of students online? When looking at the data, it's important to see the whole picture. First, data from state achievement tests are considered. These tests are the base for measurement of student success at the district, state, and national levels. Then, survey and interview feedback from the teacher's perspective is explored. You'll be interested to know upfront; they do not align. Last, consider why there is a discrepancy.

ACHIEVEMENT TEST DATA

Reading proficiency levels were compared for the entire of state of third grade students in Florida. Of all the states considered for the large-scale review, Florida was ideal. This was because Florida has Florida Virtual School (FLVS), an internet based, fully-accredited, not-for-profit, statewide public-school district. Since 1997, FLVS has served students from Kindergarten through Grade 12 with an increase in enrollment for the primary grades. FLVS also provides coursework to online programs and blended learning programs across the United States. Additionally, FLVS is a public school for the state and all state resident students are required to take the State Standards Assessments (SSA) in English Language Arts (ELA) at the same time, under the same conditions. So, there is viable data between face-to-face and virtual students to compare.

How many students are we talking about here? When looking at Florida's public school population, there are approximately 217,000 third grade students yearly who took the SSA in ELA between the school years 2014-2015 and 2020-2021. The number of third grade face-to-face students increased from 2015-2017 and then began to decrease in enrollment through 2021. The number of third grade virtual students attending FLVS increased in 2014-2015 and 2015-2016, began to decrease to its lowest in 2018-2019, 193 students, and then more than doubled in 2020-2021, reaching its highest enrollment of 449 students to date.

Figure 1

Third Grade Student State Enrollment 2015-2021

School Type	2014-2015	2015-2016	2016-2017	2017-2018	2018-2019	2020-2021
#Face-to-Face Students	215,474	220,537	227,864	221,517	216,781	198,179
#Virtual Students	280	387	369	328	193	449

Note Data source: Florida State Department of Education; data are displayed as reported in the state department of education portal

The ELA SSA data are available in the state's department of education databases as public records. Students are ranked by levels based on their performance as follows: Level 5 = Mastery, Level 4 = Proficient, Level 3 = Satisfactory, Level 2 = Below Satisfactory, and Level 1 = Inadequate. Students met the passing score on the SSA by performing at Level 3 or above. Demographic data for English Language Learners (ELLs), economic status, disability status, and race/ethnicity is also compared to gain a broader perspective of the students enrolled in both settings.

The assessment results showed steady improvement from 2015-2019 for both face-to-face and virtual students.

Virtual students outperformed face-to-face students each year and on every Level. No State Assessments were performed in the year 2020 due to the Coronavirus pandemic. The most dramatic change was in 2021 when State Assessments showed the impact COVID had on the reading levels in third grade students. Brick-and-mortar school dipped in achievement and virtual school students significantly increased (Figure 2).

Compare the Level data side by and side to see the differences. Here is the breakdown:

- 8% of face-to-face students achieved Level 5 compared to 10% of virtual students
- 20% of face-to-face students achieved Level 4 compared to 23% of virtual students
- 28% of face-to-face students achieved Level 3 compared to 31% of virtual students
- 23% of face-to-face students achieved Level 2 compared to 21% of virtual students *
- 21% of face-to-face students achieved Level 1 compared to 15% of virtual students (possible retention level) *

These students did not pass and are considered not at grade level proficiency for future success.

Overall, the number of students not reading on grade level in third grade is staggering. Forty-four percent of face-to-face students compared to 36% of virtual students did not pass the SSA in ELA between 2015-2021.

Figure 2

Third-grade State Standards Assessments Scores 2015-2021

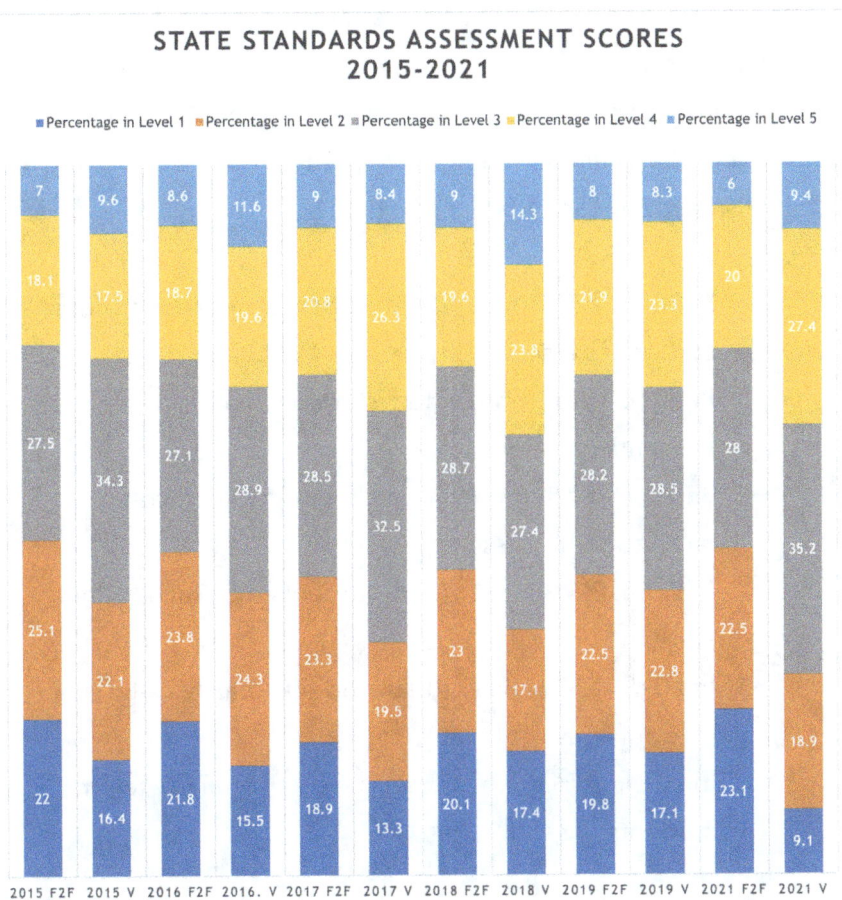

Note. F2F is for face-to-face students and V is for virtual students. Data source: data are displayed as reported in the state department of education portal

The passing rates for face-to-face third grade students and virtual third grade students performing at Level 3 and above consistently show virtual students outperforming face-to-face students. The average percentage for face-to face students is 56% compared to 64% of virtual students. This is a difference of 8% points higher overall. The most significant gap appeared in 2021 when face-to-face dipped and virtual skyrocketed, blowing the average out of the water and creating an 18% point spread. This is staggering. The breakdown per year:

- In 2015, 8.5% more virtual students than face-to-face students passed
- In 2016, 5.8% more virtual students than face-to-face students passed
- In 2017, 9.4% more virtual students than face-to-face students passed
- In 2018, 8.6% more virtual students than face-to-face students passed
- In 2019, 2.5% more virtual students than face-to-face students passed
- In 2021, 18% more virtual students than face-to-face students passed

Figure 3

Percent of Students at Level 3 or Above in SSA ELA in Years 2015-2021

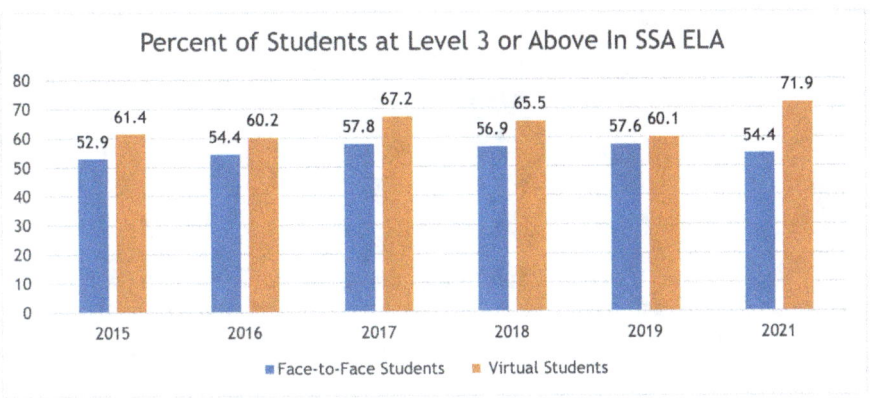

Note. Data are displayed as reported in the department of education portal; percentages may not add to 100 due to state report rounding.

In the fall of 2020, surveyed second and third grade teachers had a very different opinion about the effectiveness of virtual school. Eighty-three percent of second grade teachers felt that students were not prepared in a virtual school environment (Figure 4). Ninety percent of third grade teachers also felt that virtual school was not effective at this grade level (Figure 5). Overall, 87% of second and third grade teachers did not feel that virtual school prepared second grade students to achieve grade-level reading proficiency in third grade.

Figure 4

Second-grade Teacher Responses

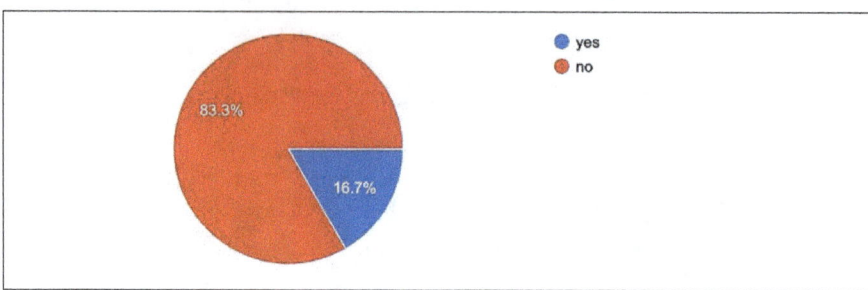

Note. Data show teachers' perceptions as to whether second-grade virtual school prepares students for third grade-level reading proficiency success (n=30).

Figure 5

Third-grade Teacher Responses

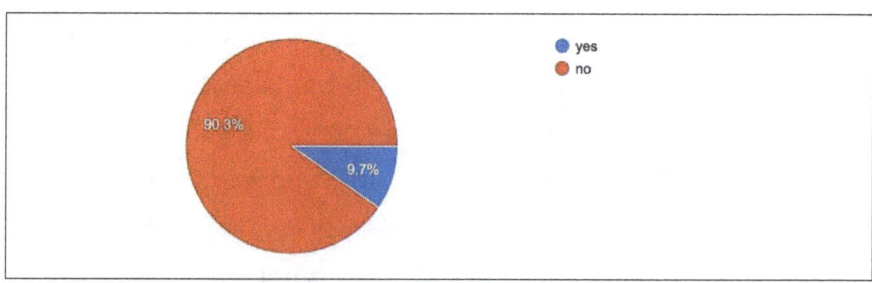

Note. Data show teachers' perceptions concerning second grade versus third-grade preparation for reading success (n=31).

Additionally, these surveyed second grade teachers were asked how they would compare the reading proficiency levels for virtual students compared to traditional face-to-face students for second grade. Hands down, at 90%, teachers felt that face-to-face students performed better than virtual students in their reading levels (Figure 6). Here is the breakdown:

- 3.3% felt that second-grade virtual school students performed better than face-to-face students in reading proficiency levels.
- 6.67% chose that virtual school students and face-to-face students performed at the same reading proficiency levels.
- 90% chose that second-grade face-to-face students performed better at reading proficiency. Most second-grade teachers thought that face-to-face students performed better than virtual school students in their reading proficiency levels.

Figure 6

Second-grade Teacher Responses

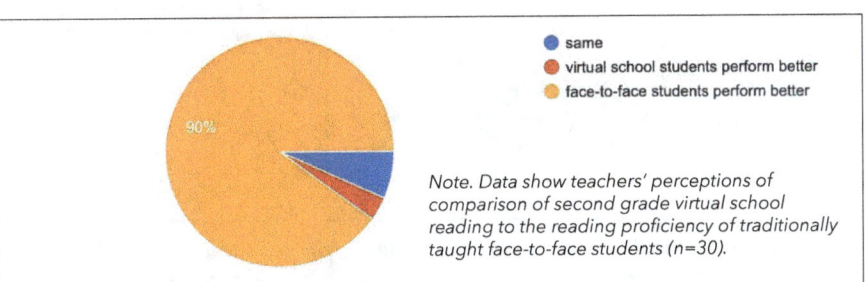

same
virtual school students perform better
face-to-face students perform better

90%

Note. Data show teachers' perceptions of comparison of second grade virtual school reading to the reading proficiency of traditionally taught face-to-face students (n=30).

Similarly, the surveyed third grade teachers were asked how third grade students who were enrolled in a virtual school for second grade performed in English Language Arts assessments compared to their peers who were enrolled in a traditional face-to-face classroom for second grade. Here is the breakdown:

- 87.1% responded that face-to face students performed better.
- 12.9% responded that the performance was the same for both groups of students.
- 0% chose that virtual school students performed better.
- Most third-grade teachers felt that students who attended a face-to-face school for second grade performed better in third grade English Language Arts assessments than students who attended a virtual school in second grade.

Figure 7

Third-grade Teacher Responses

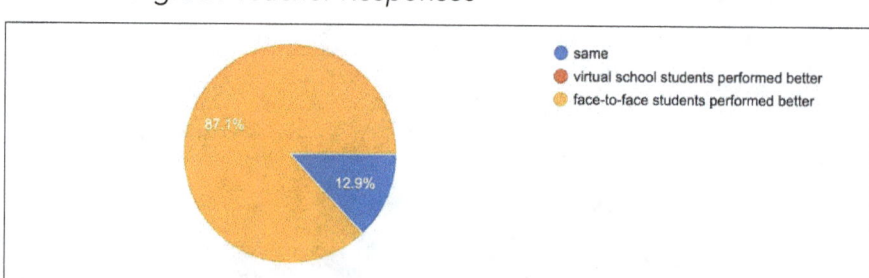

Note. Data show teachers' perceptions of how third-grade ELA students performed comparatively between second grade VS and second grade face-to-face instruction (n=31).

EQUITY

Equity in education can either widen or close opportunity gaps in society. The equity of face-to-face students and virtual students can be broken down into comparable demographic data from the Department of Education database with student achievement as well as teacher feedback through surveys and interviews. The demographic groups compared in this section are Students with Disabilities (SWD), English Language Learners (ELL), Economic Status, and Race/Ethnicity.

DISABILITY STATUS

The demographic area of disability status from 2015-2021 is students with disabilities (SWD) and students without disabilities (Non-SWD) on the SSA in ELA (Figure 8). Overall, virtual students with and without disabilities outperformed face-to-face students by 3.6% and 13.9% respectively. Here is the breakdown per year:

- In 2015, 6.6% more Non-SWD virtual students scored at Level 3 or above than Non-SWD face-to-face students, and 11.2% more SWD virtual students scored at Level 3 or above than SWD face-to-face students.
- In 2016, 2.6% more Non-SWD virtual students scored at Level 3 or above compared to Non-SWD face-to-face students, and 9.3% more SWD virtual students scored

at Level 3 or above compared to SWD face-to-face students.

- In 2017, 5.8% more Non-SWD virtual students scored at Level 3 or above compared to Non-SWD face-to-face students, and 18.8% more SWD virtual students scored at Level 3 or above compared to SWD face-to-face students.
- In 2018, 5.3% more Non-SWD virtual students scored at Level 3 or above than Non-SWD face-to-face students, and 25.9% more SWD virtual students scored at Level 3 or above than SWD face-to-face students.
- In 2019, 1.3% more Non-SWD virtual students achieved at Level 3 or above compared to Non-SWD face-to-face students, and 3% more SWD virtual students scored at Level 3 or above compared to SWD face-to-face students.
- In 2021, 15.2% more Non-SWD virtual students achieved at Level 3 or above compared to Non-SWD face-to-face students, and 15.3% more SWD virtual students scored at Level 3 or above compared to SWD face-to-face students.

Figure 8

Percent of Students at Level 3 or Above by Disability Status in Years 2015-2021

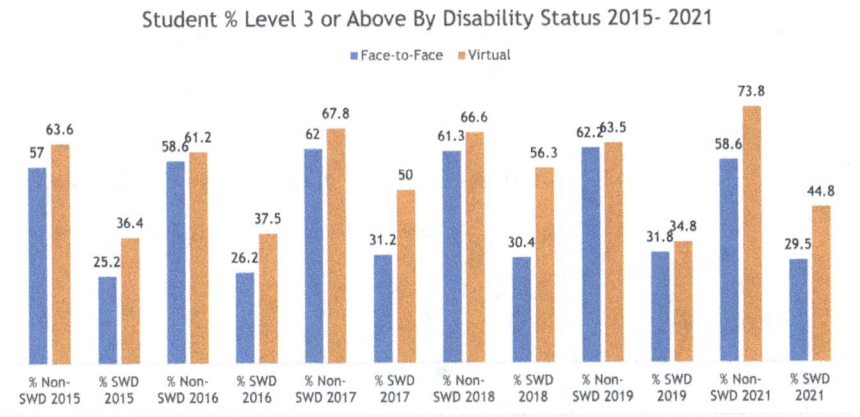

Note. Data are displayed as reported in the department of education portal.

ENGLISH LANGUAGE LEARNERS (ELL)

In 2015-2021, fewer than ten English Language Learners (ELL) took the SSA in VS and scores were not reported to protect student identity (Figure 3). Therefore, the only comparable data in the demographic area of ELL is for non-ELLs. Non-ELL virtual students outperformed non-ELL face-to-face students five out of six years (Figure 9).

- 2015- 3.9% more non-ELL virtual students scored at Level 3 or above than non-ELL face-to face students.
- 2016- 1.2% more non-ELL virtual students scored at Level 3 or above compared to non-ELL face-to-face students.

- 2017- 4.7% more non-ELL virtual students scored at Level 3 or above compared to non-ELL face-to-face students.
- 2018- 3.5% more non-ELL virtual students scored at Level 3 or above compared to non-ELL face-to-face students.
- 2019- 2.4% more non-ELL face-to-face students scored at Level 3 or above compared to non-ELL virtual students.
- 2021- 13.4% more non-ELL virtual students scored at Level 3 or above compared to non-ELL face-to-face students.

Figure 9

Percent of Students at Level 3 or Above by ELL in Years 2015-2021

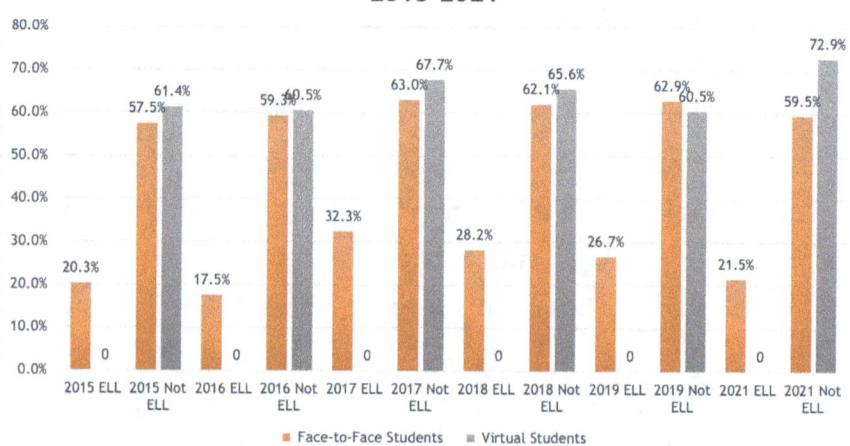

Note. Data are displayed as reported in the department of education portal; percentages may not add to 100 due to state report rounding.

ECONOMIC STATUS

The next demographic area compared was Economic Status in students with economic disadvantages and students without economic disadvantages between the years of 2015-2021 (Figure 10). Overall, disadvantaged virtual students outperformed disadvantaged face-to-face students by an average of 12.9%, and non-disadvantaged face-to-face students outperformed non-disadvantaged virtual students by an average of 6.2%.

- In 2015, 21.8% more disadvantaged virtual students scored at Level 3 or above compared to disadvantaged face-to-face students, and 12.7% more non-disadvantaged face-to-face students achieved at Level 3 or above compared to non-disadvantaged virtual students.

- In 2016, 7.2% more disadvantaged virtual students scored at Level 3 or above compared to disadvantaged face-to-face students, and 1.6% more non-disadvantaged face-to-face students achieved at Level 3 or above compared to non-disadvantaged virtual students.

- In 2017, 9% more disadvantaged virtual students scored at Level 3 or above compared to disadvantaged face-to-face students, and 0.8% more non-disadvantaged virtual students achieved at Level 3 or above compared to non-disadvantaged face-to-face students.

- In 2018, 12.6% more disadvantaged virtual students scored at Level 3 or above compared to disadvantaged face-to-face students, and 5.9% more non-disadvantaged face-to-face students achieved at Level 3 or above compared to non-disadvantaged virtual students.
- In 2019, 6.8% more disadvantaged virtual students scored at Level 3 or above compared to disadvantaged face-to-face students, and 8% more non-disadvantaged face-to-face students achieved at Level 3 or above compared to non-disadvantaged virtual students.
- In 2021, 20% more disadvantaged virtual students scored at Level 3 or above compared to disadvantaged face-to-face students, and 8.2% more non-disadvantaged virtual students achieved at Level 3 or above compared to non-disadvantaged face-to-face students.

Figure 10

Percent of Students at Level 3 or Above by Economic Status
in Years 2015-2021

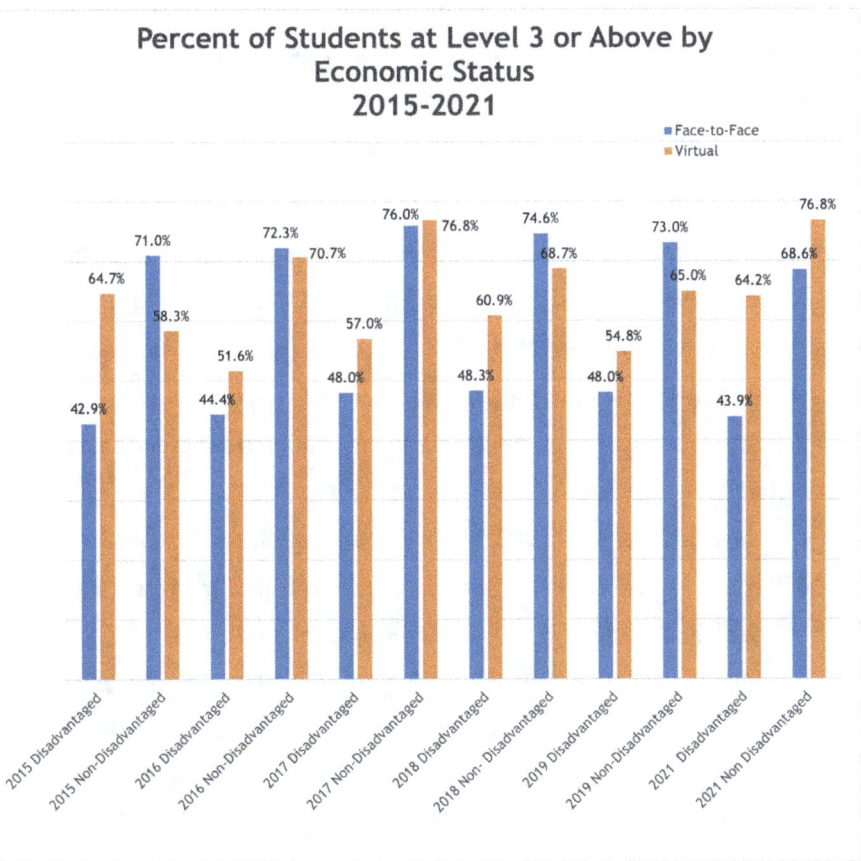

Note. Data are displayed as reported in the department of education
portal. Percentages may not add to 100 due to state report rounding.

DEMOGRAPHICS

In the last section of demographics, student race/ethnicity is compared over six years for the SSA in ELA from 2015-2021. The virtual student population of American Indian and Pacific Islander data are not shown to protect students' privacy when there are less than 10 students in a category. For four out of the five years, the virtual school Asian population was also less than ten and scores were not reported to protect students' privacy. Overall, in the remaining subgroups, the findings were that White face-to-face students outperformed White virtual students, Hispanic and Black virtual students outperformed Hispanic and Black face-to-face students, and virtual and face-to-face students of two or more races performed similarly.

Between the years 2015 and 2021, the data indicated that 4% more White face-to-face students in third grade scored at Level 3 or above on the SSA in ELA compared to the White virtual students in third grade (Figure 11). The biggest gaps swung between the years 2019 and 2021. The virtual school population of students was at its lowest in 2019 and highest in 2021.

Figure 11

Percent of White Students at Level 3 or Above 2015-2021

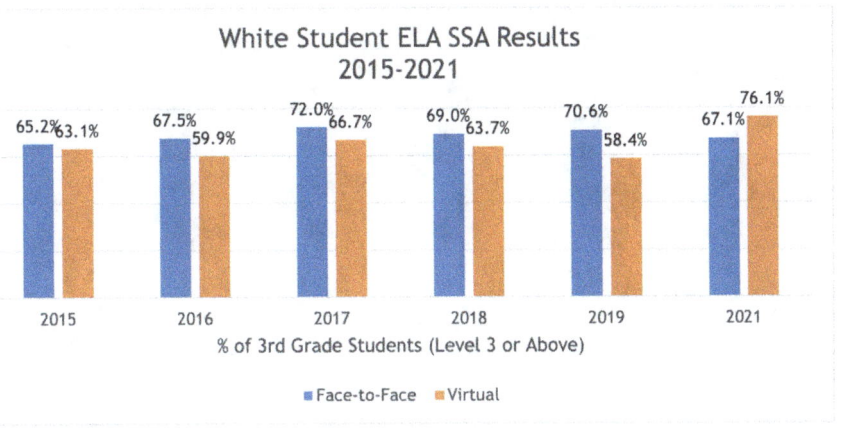

Note. Data are displayed as reported in the department of education portal.

Between the years 2015 and 2021, the data indicated that 18.4% more Hispanic virtual students in third grade scored at Level 3 or above on the SSA in ELA compared to the Hispanic face-to-face students in third grade (Figure 12). Virtual students consistently outperformed face-to-face students yearly.

Figure 12

Percent of Hispanic Students at Level 3 or Above 2015-2021

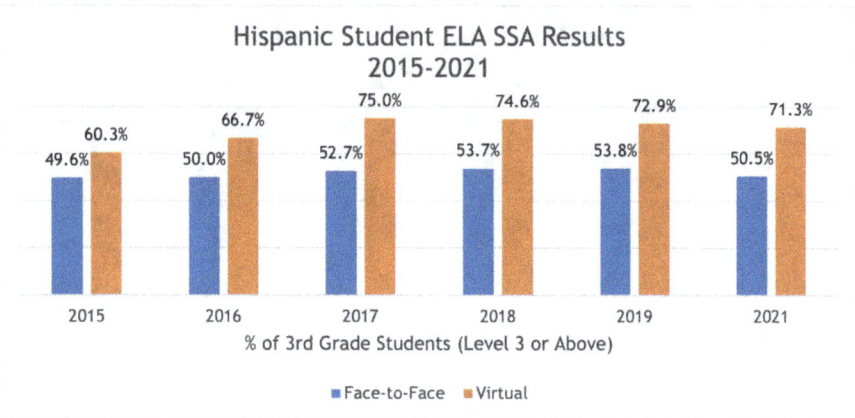

Between the years 2015 and 2021, the data indicated that 15.5% more Black virtual students in third grade scored at Level 3 or above on the SSA in ELA compared to the Black face-to-face students in third grade (Figure 13). The student achievement levels are consistent over the six-year period.

Figure 13

Percent of Black Students at Level 3 or Above 2015-2021

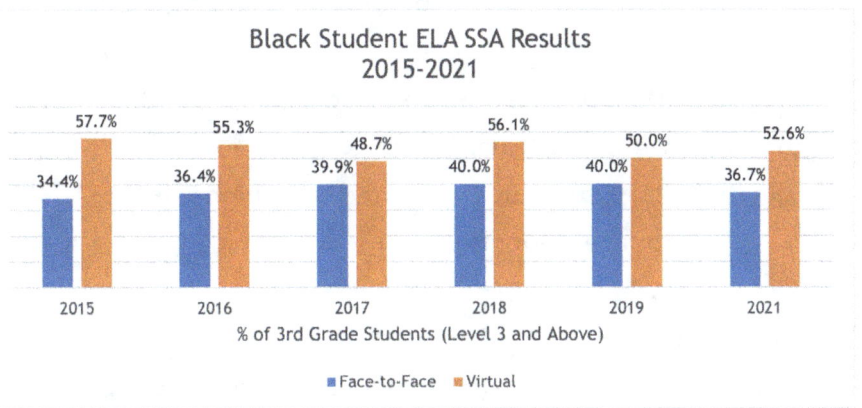

Note. Data are displayed as reported in the department of education portal.

Between the years 2015 and 2021, students with two or more races in third grade tied for overall performance (Figure 14). The data were inconsistent with either a wide gap between performance or tight and seemed to teeter totter between years. If virtual outperformed one year, face-to-face would outperform the following year at almost identical levels, yet every two years the competing levels varied. The breakdown for third grade students who scored at Level 3 or above on the SSA in ELA are as follows:

- In 2015, virtual students scored 13.5% higher than face-to-face students.
- In 2016, face-to-face students scored 12.4% higher than virtual students.

- In 2017, virtual students scored .3% higher than to face-to-face students.
- In 2018, face-to-face students scored .2% higher than virtual students.
- In 2019, face-to-face students scored 4.5% higher than virtual students.
- In 2021, virtual students scored 3.3% higher than face-to-face students.

Figure 14

Percent of Two or More Races Students at Level 3 or Above 2015-2021

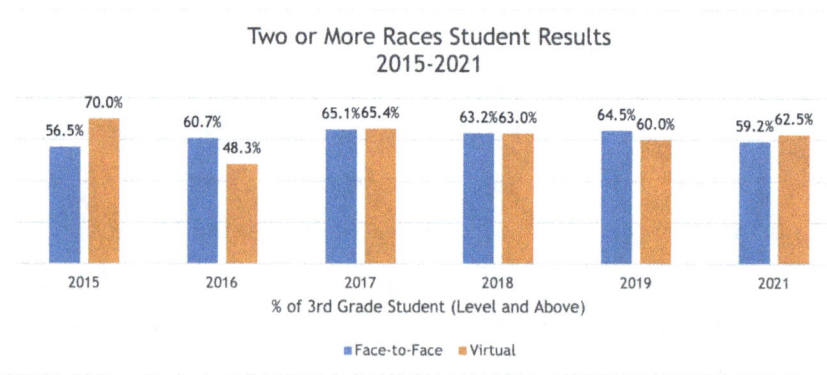

Two or More Races Student Results
2015-2021

% of 3rd Grade Student (Level and Above)

■ Face-to-Face ■ Virtual

Note. Data are displayed as reported in the department of education portal.

Surveyed second grade teachers were asked if they felt that students in a virtual second-grade school receive an equitable English Language Arts education as their peers in a traditional face-to-face school (Figure 15). Eighty percent of teachers responded no, they felt virtual and face-to-face education was not equitable. Twenty percent of teachers responded yes. Most second-grade teachers who responded to the survey did not feel that second-grade virtual students receive an equitable ELA education compared to their face-to-face peers.

Figure 15

Second-grade Teacher Responses

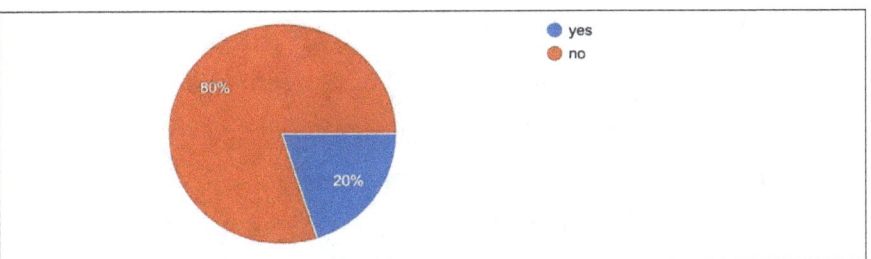

Note. Data show teachers' perceptions about whether students in a virtual second-grade school receive an equitable English Language Arts education as their peers in a traditional face-to-face school (n=30).

Surveyed third-grade teachers were asked if they felt that students in virtual second grade receive an equitable education in English Language Arts as their peers in a traditional face-to-face school (Figure 16). Ninety percent of teachers responded no, they believed that students did not receive an equitable education virtually compared to face-to-face. Ten percent of teachers felt that virtual and face-to-face student education in ELA was equitable. Most third-grade teachers felt that students who attended a virtual second grade did not receive an equitable education in English Language Arts compared to their peers in a traditional face-to-face second-grade class.

Figure 16

Third-grade Teacher Responses

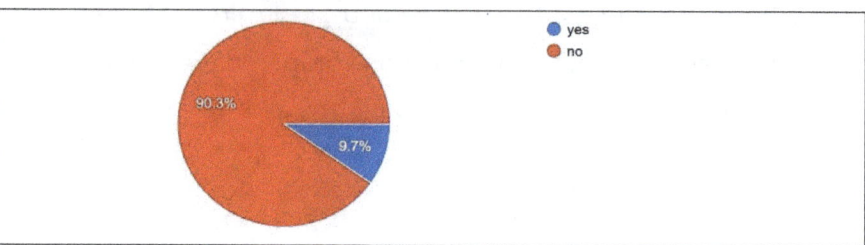

Note. Data show teachers' perception of VS versus face-to-face equitability in terms of ELA education (n=31).

The achievement gap between groups of students in school systems across the country is real. It impacts the futures of children every day. Finding a way to close this gap is imperative. A major way is to increase reading proficiency in third grade students and get them on grade level. When looking at the SSA demographic data, it is encouraging to see the raised achievement in disadvantaged, Hispanic, and Black virtual students compared to face-to-face students in the same demographic group. Virtual schools can provide a more equitable education.

Figure 17

Outperformance Summary of Percent of VS Students at Level 3 or Above in SSA ELA in Years 2015-2021

VS scored 8 percentage points higher SSA ELA scores	VS Students with Disabilities (SWD) scored 13.9 percentage points higher	VS Economically Disadvantaged students scored 12.9 percentage points higher

VS Black students scored 15.5 percentage points higher	VS Hispanic students scored 18.4 percentage points higher

Despite how teachers felt about online education, the fact remains that it works. The 2020 coronavirus pandemic pushed society into uncomfortable teaching and learning situations. However, much needed classroom advances were made. It's important to take what was learned, refine it, master it, and make a better future classroom to maximize student achievement thereby increasing reading proficiency.

Figure 18

Teacher Survey Results: Challenges and Benefits of VS

Challenges	Benefits
Teaching methods	None
Students	Better lessons
Resources	Increased access to books online
Technology	Increased student autonomy
Parents	Better enviroment

Figure 19

Teacher Survey Results 2021: Comparing VS to Face-to-Face

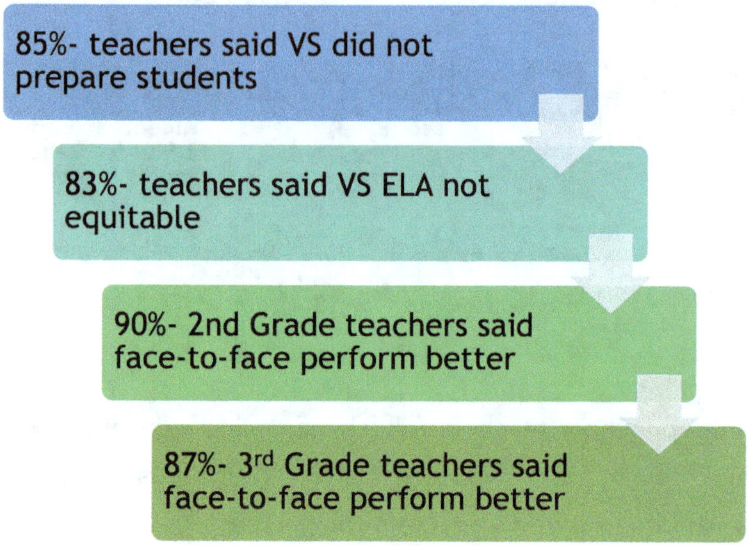

85%- teachers said VS did not prepare students

83%- teachers said VS ELA not equitable

90%- 2nd Grade teachers said face-to-face perform better

87%- 3rd Grade teachers said face-to-face perform better

Part 2

Where do we go from here?

Chapter 4:

REIMAGINING THE CLASSROOM: WHAT COVID TAUGHT US

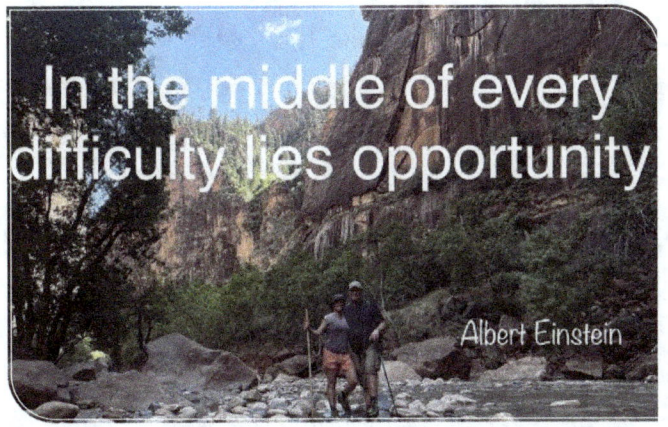

In the middle of every difficulty lies opportunity

Albert Einstein

The virtual classroom that became our learning epicenter throughout the coronavirus pandemic was a baptism by fire scenario that left few unscathed. Educational leaders walked on coals to quickly adopt a new system of learning that would meet the communities needs without having the resources. Teachers were overwhelmed by the crushing expectations to create an entire classroom using an online platform with little to no background, in record time. Students and families had to navigate a system they had never experienced and relearn how to learn, without the tools. All survived and walked away a little stronger and more tech savvy. However uncomfortable the experience of online learning was, we learned and grew as a society. We made it to the other side!

WHAT WE LEARNED

In the fall of 2020, after the initial shock and shut down of the United States' brick-and-mortar schools in the spring, teachers in Florida had a full quarter of the new 2020-2021 school year complete. The public schools started two weeks behind schedule with masks on and desks six feet apart. Some teachers were teaching face-to-face, some online, and some concurrently. Surveyed teachers were asked what benefits which affected reading proficiency they thought students had when attending a second-grade virtual school. The responses fell into five themes. *About one third of teachers, however, felt as though there were no benefits.*

1. **Better lessons-** more technology was incorporated into their lessons, greater opportunity for differentiation, focused lessons that were shorter and more specific, and less possibility of being sidetracked like in the face-to-face classroom
2. **Increased Student Autonomy-** students had more control over their work pace, could repeat materials when needed, were becoming more technologically proficient, and had better independent reading

3. **Increased Access to Books Online-** students had access to hundreds of books online and could increase exposure to cultural diversity
4. **Better Learning Environment-** fewer classroom behavior distractions, students could focus on the teacher in one-to-one environments and small groups with fewer distractions if parents provided a quiet environment, comfort of learning in their homes because "more comfortable= better performance"
5. **More Support-** parent involvement was high, more one-on-one reading time with parents, and students received more support at home increasing focus and proficiency

An interesting response was from one teacher who felt that there was much less pressure for struggling readers at home because they don't become self-conscious about their own reading if they don't have peers to compare themselves to. This concluded the virtual school benefits from second grade teacher's point of view.

Surveyed second grade teachers faced several challenges when teaching second-grade proficiency online. Their responses fell into five major themes. The most common challenges were teaching methods and students (half of teachers).

1. **Teaching methods-** difficulty scheduling one-on-one student support, small reading groups, cooperative work, and differentiation; lack of rich classroom discussions, modeling reading in-depth, observing, and listening to students interacting with text; assessing student proficiency was time consuming and difficult to accurately determine skills and deficits

2. **Students-** students struggled with focus, engagement, distractions at home, lack of discipline, consistent attendance, completion of assignments, and accountability

3. **Resources-** lack of physical books in student homes which teachers felt increased difficulty in learning to read by not being able to touch the physical book to sound out words or track text, requiring skills that students may not have yet; teachers struggled with matching synchronous materials to online books to meet student needs; lack of student access to educational software readily available in face-to-face schools

4. **Technology-** poor internet connections interfering with instruction, students had lack of access to internet, older devices, and technology issues; students and parents struggled to navigate the technology and platforms, had no training or support

5. **Parents-** inadequate student support at home with either none, too little, too much by doing work for them and helping during assessments

Surveyed teachers also felt that while teaching online, they were given no leadership, support, or training. The overwhelming challenges faced by teachers impacted feelings of adequacy and success in teaching online.

Taking what we learned from the educational crisis during the pandemic, the good and the bad, and blending it with what we knew about good teaching is the goal. School districts had to address many of these issues with devices and internet, and think flexibly for the first time about how concrete those 180 school days were with students in their seats the whole time.

No valuable change occurs without disequilibrium. It was a wonderful time for education to finally start advancing past the industrial age model we all grew up with. The problem is, it's all that people know, so change is hard not only for the teachers, but for the students, parents, and decision makers. It is difficult to support a model you have not experienced and may not understand.

THE FUTURE CLASSROOM

Flexible setting and class time during the pandemic with virtual classes allowed families to customize the school day to fit their life. Life got quiet and families focused on what was important. People questioned the norm. Learning was no longer restricted to the four walls of the classroom. Now expand and build on that.

Erase school boundary lines to create equity in school

systems. Knowledge transcends space and time. Have students tap into experts in the field of teaching regardless of location, economic status, race/ethnicity, and disability through synchronous and asynchronous classrooms. Join a live session to interact and be a part of the discussion. Recorded lessons can be viewed without limit for mastery.

Give choices for learning environments. Want a four-day school week? What about mornings at home and afternoons in the classroom? Build the routine to the schedule that allows the student to maximize their learning time. Blend learning environments. Take some classes at home virtually and some face-to-face in the classroom. Families set the schedule and partner with teachers to ensure the student's educational needs are being met. Teachers monitor and report progress.

Take activities that students are already doing and turn them into educational credit. Sports count for Physical Education class credit (soccer, basketball, tennis, swimming, etc.). Instrument practices count for Music class credit (band, orchestra, choir, etc.). The possibilities are endless. This allows for more creative flexibility in school schedules tailor-made by the family for the student.

Local availability should not limit access. The school doesn't offer the support or option your child wants or needs? No money for a speech pathologist or a special dyslexia curriculum? Join a classroom across district lines to gain access to the experts they need. Districts can work together to share the expenses. Everyone wins.

Stay home when sick. We have finally acknowledged that people get sick and need to stay home. Learning doesn't have to stop. The classroom should be accessible from home so that students are not left behind during times of illness. Teachers and parents have moved beyond the "send missed work home" to be made up later and then chasing students for the work and missed assessments. Parents are responsible for accessing their child's classroom during times of absence to ensure the lessons and work are complete and submitted electronically.

Students increased autonomy. Students became techy during COVID. With virtual classrooms, they learned how to join a video lesson, share their screens, mute, put up privacy backgrounds, access and turn in assignments and lessons electronically, and probably the most popular despite the teacher's objections, use the chat. Don't know something? You bet they know how to search and find answers using search engines and watch a video for that. Students became more independent learners on technology.

> While walking with my students, I noticed a student's shoe untied. I told him to tie it before he tripped. He said that he didn't know how. I told him that he needed to practice at home because it was important to know. I gave it to him as his "homework." He was shocked, yet didn't object.

A couple of days later, I noticed this student tying his shoes over and over again. He was very focused. I was surprised. I remarked on how well he knew how to tie them and how proud I was that he learned. I asked who helped him at home, his mother? He replied, "No, I stayed in my room and watched a YouTube video practicing all night until I could do it."

What I love about this story is that this boy took his learning into his own hands. He made the decision to learn how to tie his shoes, independently went to a source, and practiced the skill until he mastered it, without reward or monitoring.

Instruction is not one-sided. While teachers oversee and monitor the educational experience and process, in the modern classroom, students are also teachers. To allow for mastery, students must share their knowledge through demonstration, coaching, and collaboration with their peers. Students lift each other up to be the best version of themselves, allowing for empowerment. Montessori schools already capitalize on this method, and for good reason. It works.

Every morning I would start Google Classroom from my bedroom a few minutes early to say hi and allow the students to settle in. I would mute my mic, turn off my screen, and grab a coffee. I could hear the students talking to one another, parents talking in the background, and dogs barking. I felt like we were all sharing our personal lives with each other in a new way. COVID was an intimate time despite the distance.

At 9:00 sharp, I'd turn my screen back on, unmute my mic, and say good morning again, ready to begin. Remarks were made about the insane number of unicorns in the chat, a few giggles, then mics were muted, and my well-planned performance started. At the end of the lesson, I would wrap up and dismiss. I thought that was it. I was moving on to the next part of my day, parent calls.

Every day I would call a certain number of parents. Every family had their day and time. It was during these calls that I found out that one of my students, Kollyns, had organized a study group every day after my lessons to complete assignments online together. She would tell students to mute their mics when there was loud background noise, explain how to submit an assignment, clarify directions, and instruct when someone was confused. Kollyns was 8. She took charge of her learning and felt empowered. Success!

Parent conferences and teacher meetings gained virtual options. During COVID, contactless meetings were a must, but even after, it's a great option. Taking valuable time from work for parents is difficult. Teachers need substitute teachers for meetings where travel to other school buildings is necessary. Virtual conferences make meetings in small groups more personal and efficient for sharing data. Everyone's time is valuable.

These are some of the educational gains from our time in lockdown. They are a great beginning and far from where we were as a nation before COVID. Build on them.

VIRTUAL

The virtual classroom can be an exciting tailor-made learning modality. The overall experience for many has mixed reviews. It's hard to embrace a change made without consent, but it was also a forgiving time where everyone was on the same learning curve. We learned what *to do* and what *not to do*. This section is about what needs to be done to maximize learning in the virtual classroom.

The virtual classroom is different from the face-to-face classroom in many ways. For that there needs to be training. Students and parents need to learn how to learn virtually. There is a different skill set needed. Students need to learn how to manage their time very well. Parents need to assist students with this since the teacher is not in the environment with them.

In the virtual classroom, parents are the co-teachers in their child's education. Parents have to know how to navigate the learning platform, access the lessons and assessments, and submit work to support their child. They oversee the activities and ensure class requirements are being met in their home. Students need adult guidance and support, even in high school.

At the beginning of the school year, parents should join teachers for a virtual tutorial. This is important to convey information on how to navigate the learning platform, where to find classroom information, how to access the online classroom and lessons, and submit work. Parents assist their child until they are more independent and know the procedures.

Set schedules. Teachers create a schedule for synchronous lessons, when work is to be turned in, assessments, small groups, one-on-one time, and check-ins with parents. Parents create schedules for class time, work time, and reading time. Routines give students the stability of knowing what is expected of them and when, both at school and at home. Parents and teachers set a schedule for student check-ins, weekly, bi-weekly, or monthly.

On the learning platform, each subject has its own section, even Homeroom. All resources, logins, and passwords are available in each subject. Each week should be clearly labeled as a Topic with the days of the week below for easy access. All lesson descriptions, videos, and paperwork are attached to the day. Students should be able to see the current week at the top of each subject when they open it.

Student attendance and engagement in lessons is critical. If absence is unavoidable, asynchronous lessons and work should be accessible through the learning platform the same day. This way there is no lag in learning and the student is not behind the class. Distractions should be eliminated from the home during lessons. Students can wear a pair of headphones if background noise is an issue and participation is needed. The ideal location would be a quiet room with an adult within the student's line of vision. This way if there is a problem, an adult can assist.

Lessons are succinct, objective driven, and timed at student's attention spans. Clearly state the objective of the lesson with straightforward explanation, examples, and modeling. Lessons should be the length of time approximately the age of the child plus a minute or two. For example, lessons for first grade students aged 6-7, should be 7-9 minutes in length.

Lessons are recorded. Record all live synchronous lessons to be attached to the learning platform. These recorded lessons become asynchronous lessons to be accessed by absent students or to be viewed again for clarification and mastery. Do not record discussions after lessons. Think of a YouTube video you watched to learn something. The discussion after and in between can take away from the lesson, not add to it. The discussion is for those in attendance only.

Bridge the distance and reduce the isolated feeling that often comes with virtual education by participating in live discussions. The opportunity to talk with other students should occur daily in small breakout groups, as a class, or one-on-one. Teachers set times to meet with students to discuss progress. Teachers also allow for scheduled breaks for students to talk freely. This will avoid the lone wolf feeling from students, increase participation, and success.

All work should be electronically loaded to the assignment. This way all assignments are graded on the learning platform and students receive feedback quickly. Rubrics can be attached through the learning platform for all written work and projects. Transparency is important to students, parents, and teachers.

Extended periods of sitting during the virtual school day should be avoided. Be sure that students are moving, taking breaks, and following routines for work time. Like any normal school day, there are a mix of activities and stimulation to enrich and engage the student. Movement, healthy snacks, music, art, and physical education need to be a part of the virtual school day routine.

Having problems? Make sure there is an open line of communication established between teachers, parents, and students so that no one is left out of the loop and eventually behind. Everyone should know how to reach the technology support person at the school when there is an issue as well.

In summary, the virtual school day is highly organized with built in routines for maximum success. Teachers, parents, and students need to work together with open communication for this option to work successfully. Once the new skill set is acquired, the virtual classroom can offer flexibility and equity in education from the comfort of your own environment.

CONCURRENT

Concurrent classrooms have one teacher with a group of face-to-face students while other students are live streaming into the same classroom. The combined duality of the method has some benefits and drawbacks for teachers and students. Concurrent teaching was common during the pandemic, despite little to no research on its effectiveness on student success.

The strength of concurrent classrooms is that the virtual student is a part of the entire lesson from start to finish. Students see the classroom and students, even other remote students, and can be a part of the activity and discussion. If students need to be home for short periods of time due to illness or travel for instance, they can still be a part of the live learning in their classroom.

There can be weaknesses in concurrent teaching from both the teacher and student viewpoints. Some drawbacks are listed below:

- Remote students can feel left out while watching students talk and participate in the classroom.
- Students may not be able to immerse in the activities at the same level if they do not have the same materials on hand at home or printed materials ready.
- Discussions and small groups can be difficult between remote and in class students (hard for remote students to hear children speak in class).
- Engaging students at home in the same activity as the class is difficult because the teacher is splitting time between the two sets of students.
- Students in the classroom can be distracted by the backgrounds of the remote students (pets, siblings,

sounds, etc.) as it is projected in the front of the classroom.

- Teachers cannot change plans last minute or students at home will not have the ability to prepare for the lesson in time.
- Students sitting for entire school days in front of a computer screen for extended periods of time (weeks and months) can have negative effects.

Concurrent teaching was a great way to blend virtual and brick-and-mortar learning environments during the pandemic. It is also a cost-effective option for school districts to blend the virtual and face-to-face students for the price of one teacher salary. However, the cons outweigh the pros and should be considered before implementing in a school long-term.

While teaching concurrently, I saw the excitement and participation from the virtual students diminish over time. Once students got used to the routines and procedures of learning online, the loneliness set in negatively impacting their academic success. Students became depressed and began displaying atypical behavior like self-harm, letters to God with feelings of abandonment (I worked in a Catholic school), and academic stagnation or decline. Students at home felt left out and disconnected with their peers in the face-to-face environment, even with the high structure, peer dialogue, and teacher check-ins. Once virtual students returned to the face-to-face environment, their mood became positive, their normal behavior returned, and academic success increased.

BLENDED LEARNING

Blended learning uses a combination of virtual classes and face-to-face classes. This combination offers flexibility to students and gives schools the ability to consolidate resources with other schools, districts, and adjunct professionals. To better meet students' needs, a virtual learning lab can bridge student access to high quality education and create equity in the school system.

Students remain a part of their face-to-face cohort class and use the virtual learning lab like a library. Brick-and-mortar schools can use this virtual learning lab to give various students access to a virtual class or resource they do not have while giving student support. Teachers monitor the virtual school lab during the day to ensure that students are safe and on task.

Using the blended learning model, students gain access, flexibility, and support. Students come to brick-and-mortar school during the day and use the virtual learning lab for online classes when needed. Student academic success would increase using this blended model of virtual learning labs inside the brick-and-mortar school building.

Chapter 5:

ENVISIONING CHANGE, A PLAN FOR EDUCATION LEADERS

———————

COVID didn't just focus on our nation's reading problem, it gave us part of a solution. It's up to policy makers to use what we learned from the experience with teaching online and advance the educational system. It is time to include distance education as a valid partner for the future.

Virtual education has proven to be a viable contender in teaching reading fluency to children in the primary grades. What are the facts?

- Third grade Virtual School students outperformed brick-and-mortar students by an average of 8 percentage points on the English Language Arts State Standards Assessments from 2015-2021 (no data 2020).
- Third grade Virtual School students outperformed brick-and-mortar students by an average of 18 percentage points on the English Language Arts State Standards Assessments in 2021.
- Third grade Virtual School students outperformed brick-and-mortar students within demographic groups such as Hispanic, Black, Students With Disabilities (SWD), and Economically Disadvantaged by as much as 20 percentage points.
- The DOE data did not correlate with the data in the teachers' surveys and interviews.
- According to the survey data, 85% of second and third grade teachers felt that virtual school did not prepare second-grade students to achieve grade-level reading proficiency in third grade.
- Interviewed teachers had concerns and faced many challenges teaching reading proficiency to second-grade students virtually.

The current conditions in education have never been more ready to embrace online learning. School districts have already invested in the technology and infrastructure needed to maintain virtual classrooms. While not perfect, the hardest hurdle has been to overcome mindset. We now know that it works and that we can do it. Virtual classrooms give the education system flexibility at the elementary levels that was not present on such a large scale before.

Leap ahead with faith. Education needed to be forced to make large-scale changes. Do not allow educators and schools to revert back to the tried and true methods. Blend what we learned to make it better. It starts with what we train our teachers in.

The biggest challenge was that teachers and leaders who moved from face-to-face educational environments to virtual education environments during the coronavirus pandemic had insufficient knowledge in virtual teaching and learning theories and strategies. Teaching is heavily rooted in face-to-face traditions and theories. Teacher training is based on face-to-face strategies and methodologies. Therefore, there was a lack of knowledge among teachers for what good virtual teaching and learning looked like. Some major challenges the surveyed and interviewed teachers reported facing were in their teaching methods. Teachers did not know how to teach virtually, as they were never trained to do so.

In order for teachers and students to be on a level

playing field, all teachers need to have a solid foundation in online teaching and learning methods in their university teacher training. COVID proved that all teachers need this knowledge, not just the select few who went for a higher degree to specialize in it. At any time, teachers can be assigned a virtual classroom within the brick-and-mortar setting. The emergency DIY methods, like watching Simple K-12 and Google Classroom videos, got educators through temporarily, but it also created bad teaching habits that need to be overwritten.

ONLINE TEACHING EDUCATOR POLICY

Teachers need to have online education training. The Online Teaching Educator Policy can occur in two prongs. The first prong requires preservice teachers at every level to have three semester hours in the area of online teaching and learning. The second prong requires all inservice teachers to have professional development in three semester hours or 60 inservice points in the area of online teaching and learning. Inservice teachers will have one year from the day and month assigned an online student to complete the professional development. Inservice teachers without an online student assigned to their classroom will have two years to complete the three semester hours or 60 inservice points required. Teachers will submit documentation of required completion to the Certification office at the state's department of education office. Teachers not meeting the requirement will be out-of-field, meaning that they are qualified to teach only what their professional certificate indicates, but not in the online version of any subject area.

There needs to be a change in leadership plan focused on creating a teacher training alignment between the state university education degree programs and school district professional development for online education to create a culture shift that includes a virtual education program as part of every brick-and-mortar school. Teachers and students will have the option to teach and learn online. Online teachers will instruct online students from brick-and-mortar schools. Students will have flexible schedules to take the ELA class online from home with a choice to rejoin the face-to-face class for the rest of the day to allow for socialization. Another student option will be to join an ELA online classroom in the brick-and-mortar school, requiring no transportation or childcare issues for families. This online classroom will be for multiple grade levels and monitored by one teacher. Teacher knowledge in online education combined with the option of ELA virtual education in every school will provide an equitable ELA education to increase reading achievement.

Figure 20

Recommendation Rationale

Policy requiring all teachers in the state under study to have online teaching and learning training.

- Teachers did not feel prepared
- Teachers felt the ELA education was inequitable
- Teacher data contradicts DOE data
- Lack of training impacted student achievement in reading proficiency

The policy will effectively address low student reading proficiency by allowing more students to receive an equitable ELA education online by teachers trained in online teaching and learning, as demonstrated by the data from the VS students from 2015-2021. Online teaching and learning training for teachers benefits both teachers and students. Teachers will have more flexibility in their teaching assignments by being prepared to effectively educate students in both face-to-face and virtual classrooms with research-based methods of instruction. In addition, students who cannot attend school face-to-face will have an ELA education that is equitable to their face-to-face peers.

The ideal context is that all students will read proficiently in third grade regardless of race, ethnicity, ELL status, ESE status, socioeconomic factors, and technology access. Politicians need to advocate ELA virtual education in second grade as a viable option to increase reading proficiency because it has proven to be more effective than face-to-face learning. Virtual education will create equitable education opportunities in ELA for all students.

The department of education leaders need to financially support virtual education as a viable learning option for students of all ages by allocating state funding to required teacher training in online education and the technology needed to operate online classrooms within already established brick-and-mortar schools. Virtual education has the ability to save school districts money by having more students perform on grade level and requiring fewer school services. Ultimately, more students will succeed in high school and graduate on time to move onto successful careers.

Teachers and school district leaders will increase their perceived value of virtual education and include it in strategic plans to increase reading proficiency. Students, parents, and community members will become aware of the effectiveness of virtual education in second grade as a viable option to increase student achievement in third grade reading proficiency and access its available resources, making ELA education more equitable.

ECONOMIC ANALYSIS

There is an economic impact of a policy proposal requiring all teachers to be trained in online teaching and learning on three levels: students, community, and school districts. The first level is the students. Hernandez reported that "Children who do not read proficiently by the end of third grade are four times more likely to leave school without a diploma than proficient readers."[26] In addition, high school dropouts have an earning potential of half of what a student who completed a bachelor's degree or higher degree would earn, which directly impacts their economic self-sufficiency.[27] Implementing this policy will increase student

---

[26] D. J. Hernandez(2012). *Double jeopardy: How third-grade reading skills and poverty influence high school graduation.* The Annie E. Casey Foundation.
[27] L. Fiester (2010). *Early warning! Why reading by the end of third grade matters.* In Annie E. Casey Foundation (pp. 1–62). https://www.aecf.org/resources/earlywarning-why-reading-by-the-end-of-third-grade-matters/

achievement in reading proficiency, positively impact high school graduation rates and the future socioeconomic status of students.

The second level that the policy proposal will impact economically is the community. Teachers trained in online teaching and learning will use research-based methods for improving instruction in ELA to increase student achievement in reading proficiency. Increased ELA scores on the SSA will increase the school's rating as assigned by the state department of education based upon student outcomes on the SSA. Families will feel that they are getting the best education for their children, which will increase the number of families who want to send their children to the local public school, thereby increasing the property value in the community. School success impacts the community it serves.

The third level of the economic impact of the policy for trained teachers in online teaching and learning is the school districts. Sherrill Waddell studied the effectiveness of virtual school size and its impact on student achievement, and she advocated for virtual schools as a cost-effective way to educate students.[28] Virtual School (VS) is a free option and a public school in the state under study, directly competing with brick-and-mortar public schools for students. In 2018-2019, it cost $1,715.16 less per student per year to educate in VS than brick-and-mortar schools. Additionally, school

---

[28] S. Waddell (2017). Examining the relationship between virtual school size and student achievement. *Quarterly Review of Distance Education, 18*(4), 23–35.

districts will save money by not building as many brick-and-mortar schools. Flexible schedules and shared office space by teachers can better utilize existing buildings and stop the growing need to build. The state politicians need to change how they fund school district capital building and allocate monies to include online training for inservice teachers and the technology needed to support virtual education in brick-and-mortar public school districts.

Funding for professional development by the school district can come from Title II Part A: Supporting Effective Instruction in the Every Student Succeeds Act. My policy proposal aligns with the purpose of Title II because it will improve teacher preparation programs in quality and effectiveness within the state to increase student academic achievement in ELA. The department of education decision-makers in the state under study will need to apply for Part B: National Activities portion of the Title II funding from the U. S. Department of Education and provide a description of my policy plan to improve equitable access to effective teachers.[29]

---

[29] NASSP. (2021). National Association of Secondary School Principals. www.nassp.org

Chapter 6:

ENVISIONING SUCCESS, A PLAN FOR TEACHERS

Teachers when asked to reflect on their time teaching online...

When looking forward, it's incredibly satisfying to look back and see the hurdles teachers have overcome. After all, growth comes through reflection. In this section, teachers take stock on where they've been and how to continue to develop the skills gained to increase reading proficiency in students.

Some of the most laughable and frustrating moments came through teaching online. While students' homes opened up to the virtual classroom, everyone became a little closer. Pets, siblings, cousins, grandparents, and parents were all part of the virtual classroom community and every day felt like it was Pajama Day. Getting down to business and keeping students engaged became a struggle against the multitude of home distractions. While one student entertained the class with the peek-a-boo session from his bed, another rode his stick horse in the background, a girl popped up from the pool to answer a question, and a bikini clad mom bent over the camera to find out what kind of sauce her child wanted with her chicken nuggets. What was seen could not be unseen. So how did anyone learn? There was no reset button. Learning to fly the plane while flying it became the high-stress norm.

It's no surprise to find out that most teachers left virtual teaching with a sour taste in their mouths. Most believed that online learning flat-out didn't, doesn't, and could never replace face-to-face teaching. Who could blame them after the chaos they experienced? The fact remains however, that when done correctly, with teachers, students, and parents all working together, virtual school did outperform face-to-face instruction in English Language Arts from 2015-2021. That's a long run. We need to understand why.

To begin with, something must be done to change the way teachers are prepared for certification, starting at the university level. Then it's time to play catch-up with the teacher achievement gap in the country created because universities did not believe teachers needed online teaching training to prepare them for the future classroom. Teachers can also use this knowledge to enhance their face-to-face instruction to help increase reading fluency, by maintaining a transparent objective-driven reading class that parents and students can access at any time.

TEACHER TRAINING

The proposed online teaching and learning course and professional development will include Michael G. Moore's Theory of Transactional Distance (TD) as a pedagogical concept to describe teaching procedures and learner behaviors in distance education.[30] His theory supports the increase in student achievement in distance education by reducing TD. Increased TD between learners and teachers reduces student achievement. Moore breaks TD into three areas, referred to as clusters. These clusters are Instructional Dialogue, Program Structure, and Learner Autonomy. Teachers will learn the theory of TD and apply his methods to reduce TD in their online classrooms and improve student achievement.

The social impacts of a teacher training policy proposal in online teaching and learning will increase engagement between teachers, students, and parents. Moore stated in his original theory that distance education "Is a concept describing the universe of teacher-learner relationships that exist when learners and instructors are separated by space and/or time." His Theory of Transactional Distance (TD) describes this psychological and communications space

---

[30] M. Moore (1997). Theory of transactional distance. In D. Keegan (Ed.), *Theoretical principles of distance education* (pp. 22–38). Routledge.

that profoundly affects teachers and learners, which leads to special teacher and learner behaviors. Moore recommended six processes to be structured in every distance educational course. Training in Moore's theory of TD is the cornerstone of teacher education in online teaching and learning policy in an effort to reduce TD and improve student achievement.

Additionally, Xiaoxia Huang et al. created an instrument for measuring transactional distance in online courses in 2015, which proved to be useful for improving online course design.[31] Huang et al.'s TD measuring instrument will be part of the required teacher training to improve online course design and instruction methods. Another component to teacher education will be the findings of the research in 2016 by Huang et al. which address online learning environments with newer types of instructional media and changing learner demographic attributes.[32] Online teachers will incorporate the suggestion by Huang et al. that online instruction should include high dialogue and high structure, synchronous communication tools, and require students' discussion to reduce TD.

Huang et al. conducted two studies to research the validity of Moore's theory of TD related to distance courses today. Huang et al. developed and validated a measuring instrument of TD, which proved helpful in improving the

---

[31] X. Huang, Chandra, A., DePaolo, C., Cribbs, J., & Simmons, L. (2015). Measuring transactional distance in web-based learning environments: an initial instrument development. *Open Learning, 30*(2), 106–126

[32] X. Huang, Chandra, A., DePaolo, C. A., & Simmons, L. L. (2016). Understanding transactional distance in web-based learning environments: An empirical study. *British Journal of Educational Technology, 47*(4), 734–747. https://doi.org/10.1111/bjet.12263

future online course design and instruction methods to bridge the psychological and communications space. Through an empirical study, Huang et al. provided evidence to support Moore's theory of TD as applicable to current online environments with newer types of instructional media and changing learner demographic attributes. Second, Huang et al. addressed the impacts of the constructs of dialogue, structure, and learner autonomy in TD and found that high dialogue (+D) and high structure (+S) led to the least perceived TD. They suggested that online instructors use +D+S, synchronous communication tools, and require student discussions to reduce TD. Huang et al. warned that special attention needed to go to the students required to take online courses but preferred face-to-face courses and found that students aged 25 and older were more autonomous than students aged 18-24. Gulnara M. Burdina et al. supported Moore and Huang et al. with his study of 430 eight and nine-year-old online students. Burdina et al. found that students need socialization and that a course structure with +D+S made a significant improvement in student achievement in a virtual school learning environment.[33]

The teacher training policy will impact the social relationships between students and parents as well. Parents will spend more time with their child supporting their education, increasing student and parent interaction, and raising academic achievement. Second-grade teachers

---

[33] G. M. Burdina, Krapotkina, I. E., & Nasyrova, L. G. (2019). Distance learning in elementary school classrooms: An emerging framework for contemporary practice. *International Journal of Instruction, 12*(1), 1–16.

in my survey felt that students received better support, affecting reading proficiency when attending a virtual school. Surveyed teachers also stated that students had a better focus with parent support, parent support was high, and students may have received more one-on-one reading time with parents. Heidi Curtis and Loredana Werth found that "Student achievement in online classes is affected by the performance of the school, students, and parents."[34] Curtis and Werth interviewed parents of online students and found that communication should be to both parents and students. They found that parents wanted better communication on available resources to engage in school more effectively to avoid student failure. The transparency of online classes through the Learning Management System (LMS) was appreciated by the interviewed parents and gave them the knowledge they needed to assist their children. This policy will train teachers in online course design and how to properly manage Learning Management Systems to improve communications with students.

DO THIS NOW!

Teachers need to have online teaching and learning skills, regardless of their current position. These skills are completely transferrable to face-to-face instruction, will enhance student learning and make instruction more efficient long-term. Start this for the first day of school and

---

[34] H. Curtis, & Werth, L. (2015). Fostering student success and engagement in a K-12 online school. *Journal of Online Learning Research, 1*(2), 163–190.

keep it updated as part of weekly lesson planning. Use it to teach from daily. Teachers will always be ready for face-to-face, virtual, concurrent, blended, absent students, or even substitute teachers. By considering the research in online education and teachers' experiences, classrooms can and will be more versatile if educators follow these four areas of focus:

1. Design Online Classroom
2. Use Online Instruction Methods
3. Consider Student Attributes Online
4. Set and Maintain Consistent Communication

Figure 21

Four Focus Areas for Teachers

DESIGN ONLINE CLASSROOM

When designing the online classroom, start with the big picture in mind: backwards design format, resources, and transparency. This is the bridge between parents and teachers. Use the backwards design for class setup, section topics by week, and use electronic forms and rubrics for assessments. Having this online platform available for students and parents ensures that no lesson is ever missed and concepts can be reviewed for mastery, even from home. Reading skills can be mastered and increased this way.

Use a backwards design for each separate class. Keep it simple and easy, but also pay attention to the details. Each skill and assessment are tied into the standards and objectives of the class. Use a straightforward format for students. Think, what will they be doing in this class? What do they need now? Do not overwhelm with too much all at once.

In each class, organize topics by the week with the current week always on top and labeled. In each week, label the day and focus skill. An example is given below (Figure 22) of a weekly schedule in Reading. It will keep you and the students organized. Each day, detail the lesson and attach all resources: links, documents, and rubric. An example is given in Figure 23 of the weekly skill focus and skills in Reading.

Figure 22

Example: Weekly Topic Organized

Reading Jan. 24th-28th

📖	Mon. Story and Skills	Posted Jan 19
📖	Tues. Suffixes and Centers	Edited Jan 25
📖	Wed. To Be Verbs and Centers	Posted Jan 19
📖	Thurs. Character and Centers	Posted Jan 19
📋	Fri. Reading Story	Due Jan 28

Figure 23

Example: Daily Lesson, Reading

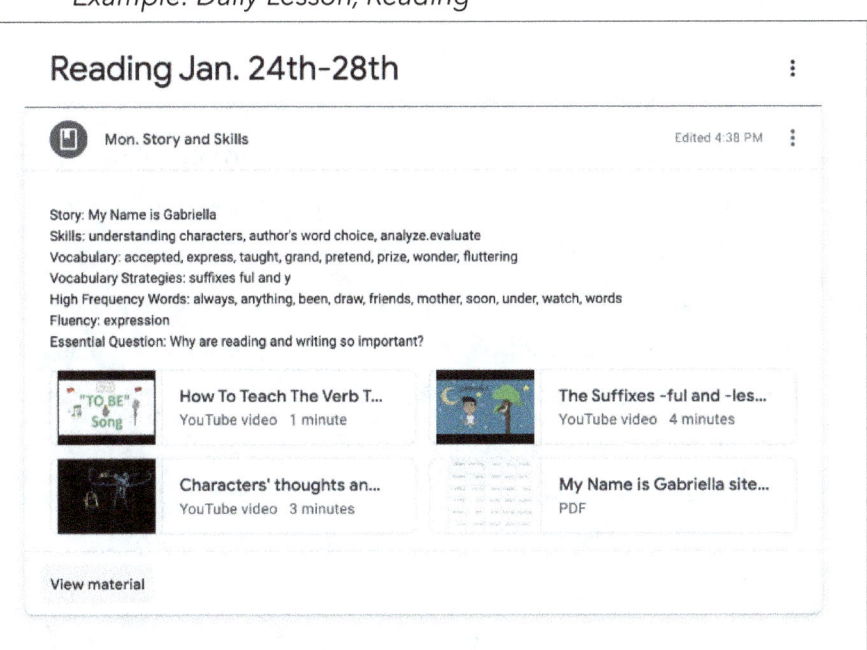

Reading Jan. 24th-28th

📖 Mon. Story and Skills — Edited 4:38 PM

Story: My Name is Gabriella
Skills: understanding characters, author's word choice, analyze.evaluate
Vocabulary: accepted, express, taught, grand, pretend, prize, wonder, fluttering
Vocabulary Strategies: suffixes ful and y
High Frequency Words: always, anything, been, draw, friends, mother, soon, under, watch, words
Fluency: expression
Essential Question: Why are reading and writing so important?

How To Teach The Verb T... — YouTube video 1 minute
The Suffixes -ful and -les... — YouTube video 4 minutes
Characters' thoughts an... — YouTube video 3 minutes
My Name is Gabriella site... — PDF

View material

Use electronic forms for easy submission and grading. Online assessments allow for immediate feedback and high engagement when students can see what they got right and wrong right away. This can be for tests and rubrics. An example of an online assessment in the daily lesson is given in Figure 24.

Figure 24

Example: Electronic Assessment

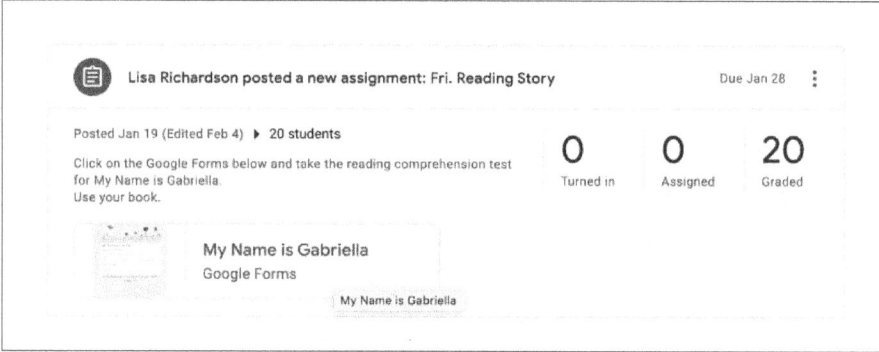

Resources keep everything running smoothly, allowing students and parents easy access at any time. Elementary school teachers will need to use the subject Homeroom to store all your basic information like class lists, teacher bio, expectations/syllabus, etc. (Figure 25). For each class, subject, add a topic named Resources and place it on the bottom of the coursework section (Figure 26). Place all the class electronic books, remedial resources, enrichment resources, recurring forms, and even passwords here.

Figure 25

Example: Homeroom

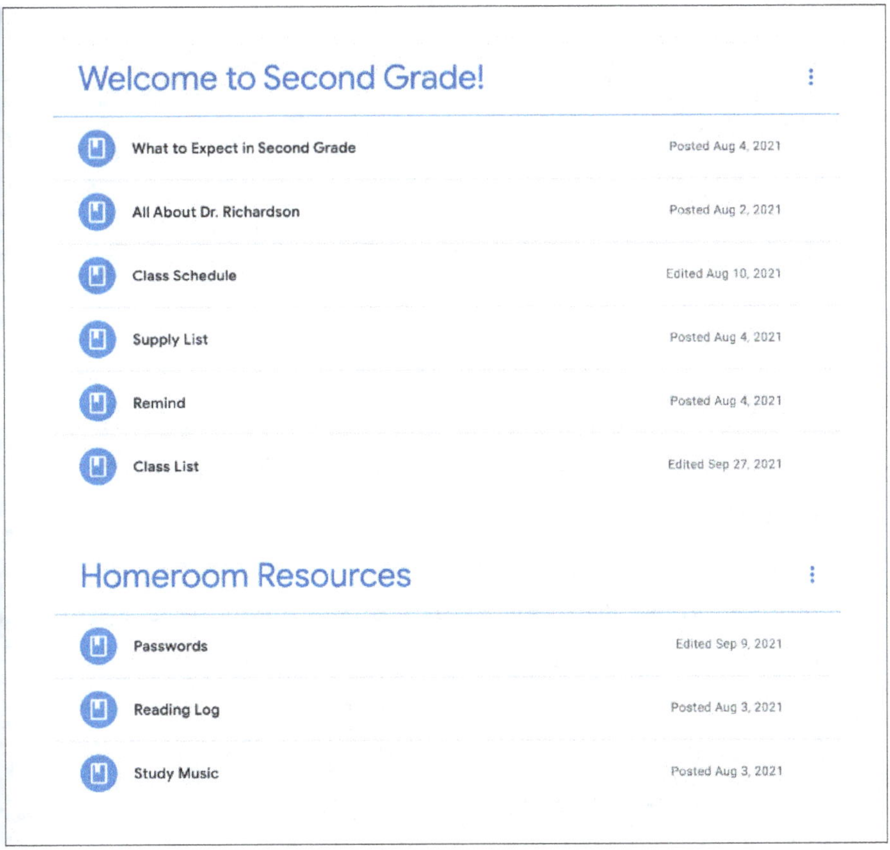

Figure 26

Example: Reading Resources

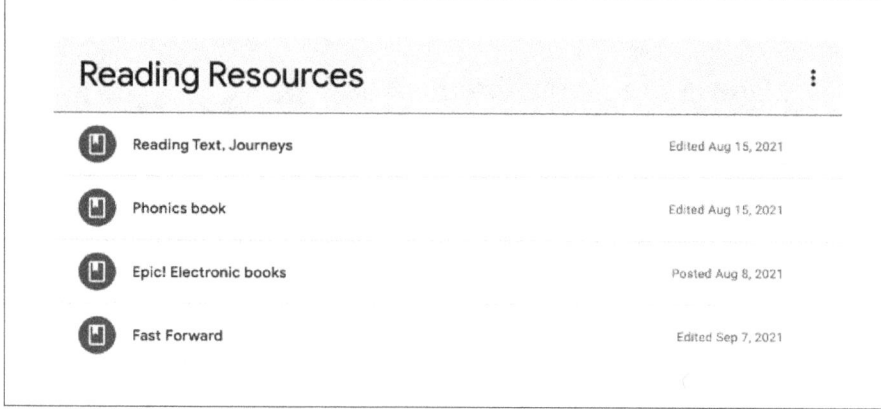

Transparency increases student success. When all lessons, assessments, and grading are done online, transparency will be your friend. If a student is absent, they never miss the information, whether out of town or sick. They can access it from wherever they are, whenever they can and submit assessments and assignments. Grading and feedback can be done electronically as well. Electronic submissions also allow for more transparency in the form of documentation. This is a good way to keep parents informed and up to date with reading milestones so that they can partner with you when needed. An example is given in Figure 27 of a writing submission and rubric assessment.

Figure 27

Example: Writing Submission and Rubric

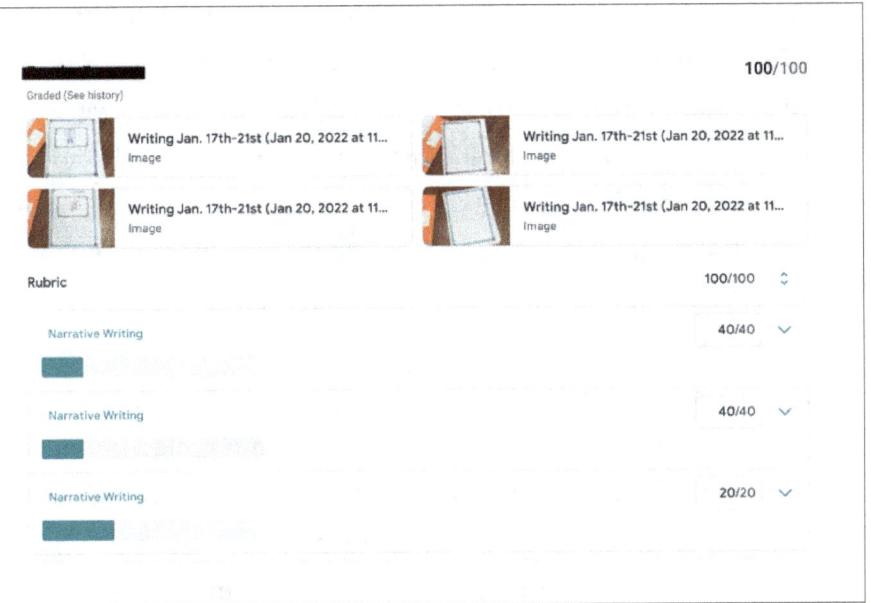

Before you know it, the year will be over and you will have a rich collection of lesson plans ready to access and share for the following year by using these online class design procedures. Online learning management systems keep teachers organized with lesson plans, videos, worksheets, and materials in a visually appealing format. In case of absences, subs, students, and parents can all access the plans and materials online as well. The ease to upload assignments and grade assessments allows for flexible time management, student accountability, and transparency.

USE ONLINE INSTRUCTION METHODS

When instructing online use the methods of high structure, limited lecture times, and high dialogue. Keep these three areas in mind when planning your lessons. Online classes are different than face-to-face in that you cannot ever wing it and there is a time limit. Using these methods will also enhance your face-to-face classroom instruction.

To begin, or before you begin, set the weekly and daily class schedules, then stick to them as much as humanly possible. It allows students to be prepared and comfortable. Teachers must have the lesson ready to go with objective, lecture, activity, and wrap-up in the learning management platform at least a day before. Set routines and procedures, just like in the face-to-face classroom, paying close attention to not waste any time online. Part of the high structure is that the use of time is succinct and flows. It takes more up-front time to set up but pays off during and after.

This leads to the second step, lesson time. Set your lecture time to the age of the student plus one minute, with a ten-minute limit. If the lecture needs more than 10 minutes, break it into chunks with discussion and activities in between to check for understanding. Keep it direct and simple. Enhance with visuals and music. When teaching live lessons (synchronous), record the lecture and post to the lesson online (asynchronous) for students to access later. This is great for students who were absent, review for a test, or watching again to improve understanding. Do not record discussions, it is too long for students to sit, and they will most likely lose interest. You lose more than you gain.

The third focus in instruction methods is high dialogue. High dialogue with student discussions increases student success. After each lecture, an activity that includes student discussion is a must. You can maximize this using breakout sessions so that all students have the opportunity to talk and not be limited to a select few students that usually answer the teacher questions. Teachers then drop in on these small groups just like they would in class, only the students don't know when the teacher will drop in, so it keeps students on their toes to continue the discussion. Limit the time ahead of time so that students know, and the alarm will alert them and bring them back to the full online classroom. Assign a group captain to report back to the class each time and mix groups up for diversity. Class polls are another great way to engage and gather data when checking for understanding. Reaching the lesson objective is key.

CONSIDER STUDENT ATTRIBUTES ONLINE

Students learn differently online just as they do face-to-face, so it's important to recognize how you will reach everyone. Besides using a mixed method with assignments, activities, and projects, students need two things to keep them on track; built in socialization time and extra attention if they prefer face-to-face instruction.

Research has shown that even with a high structure and

high dialogue classroom, students need socialization to be built into their day while learning online. A large part of the brick-and-mortar day is built around student socialization. Students who were remote during COVID showed signs of depression and loneliness. Recognizing socialization as an innate human need is important to student success. Therefore, make a part of the day online a place where students can talk freely. This is not lesson time, but rather a free time to share their pets, accomplishments, etc. that is adult monitored. It could be a 15-minute lunchtime or "recess." Either way, schedule it, and use it.

When students are not autonomous and struggle with remote learning, schedule time to check in and talk with them. It may be as simple as staying online for five extra minutes after each class when the rest of the students have been dismissed and logged off. Another option is to allow for study groups to stay online and work together after class. Organically formed groups are best because they have a natural leader, but if none naturally occur, bring it up as a suggestion in class and follow up. Students working together allow for mastery and learning in a different way than when the teacher led.

SET AND MAINTAIN CONSISTENT COMMUNICATION

Communication should be with both students and parents for maximized student achievement. Start with learning platform training with both groups together, have a class app for parents to join, and then set up a check-in schedule. Having communication upfront and throughout the year will ensure students are on track and stay there.

Learning management platform training needs to be with students and parents before the first day of school. The processes of logging in, accessing lessons, submitting assignments, reading feedback, and keeping track of the schedule is new to everyone. Parents didn't learn this way, so they need to know what your expectations are as a teacher and how to support their child.

Take the time to have group training on the learning platform and record it. Upload the training tutorials to answer questions like, how do I upload an assignment, in the Homeroom class or resource section of the class. This way, they can go back at any time. It's common to have an information overload during these training sessions. Spend time the first couple of weeks during class to show students, even in the face-to-face classroom. Use it daily. It takes time and repetition to build new habits.

Choose a class app like Remind or Class Dojo and ensure that parents join this app during their training. Add the information to join like codes, in the class Homeroom as well. This will allow teachers to send out announcements, have group messaging, and exclusive messages without parents having teacher's phone numbers. Teachers can send parents pictures of students learning throughout the day in face-to-face classrooms as well so that they feel connected to their child's learning environment.

Set up a schedule with parents of online students to check-in via video conference, telephone, or text messaging before the first day of class. Limit the check-in time to five minutes and be sure to keep it. If parents know it will be quick, but that you will check in every week, they will be more likely to answer and keep to the schedule. Recognizing that everyone has busy schedules, that time is valuable, and by respecting parent's time, will keep it quick as well. If every day there are five calls, then check-ins can be done within a half hour daily. Check-ins give online classrooms one-on-one human contact and make sure no student is falling behind.

Educators need to be ready for face-to-face, concurrent, blended, or virtual teaching roles at any time. Having online teaching and learning skills will not only enhance a teacher's classroom but will increase reading fluency. Start by focusing on these four main areas: Design Online Classroom, Use Online Instruction Methods, Consider Student Attributes Online, and Set and Maintain Consistent Communication. Implement them into the classroom to be ready for just about anything. Being prepared is the key.

Chapter 7:

ENVISIONING CONTROL, A PLAN FOR PARENTS

The world as we have created it is a process of our thinking. It cannot be changed without changing our thinking.

Albert Einstein

Have you ever looked back at your life and thought to yourself, *I wish I would have known that before...?* As a parent, life is a fast-paced, juggling act that comes with no guidebook. If there was, there would be a big star next to what you should know before your child starts off to their first day in kindergarten, and that is just how important it's going to be to keep on top of their reading progress. This section will guide you on knowing what to expect for reading milestones kindergarten-second grade, what to do if your child doesn't reach a reading milestone, and how to support your child for online learning and reading success.

Research shows that there is a limited window for reading instruction success in students to reach their maximum potential. The longer it takes for a child to learn how to read, the wider the academic gap becomes and stays. Students that are behind in kindergarten usually stay behind. Each subsequent school year interventions are put into place, they become less effective, plateauing in second grade to an almost flatline in third grade. Therefore, the faster a reading problem is detected and diagnosed; the faster your child will get the help they need.

Remember, the goal is to read on grade level in third grade for on-time high school graduation, college readiness, and career success. To be clear, if your child is not reading on grade level in third grade, they never will. This is because in kindergarten through second grade students learn to read. Starting in third grade, students read to learn.

As mother of four, I could not have guessed the ranges in ability I would face. As a teacher, school always came easily to me. Growing up I thought that was how it was for everyone, and it even continued when my two oldest started school. But then my third son came along and had a vastly different experience.

My third child struggled in a way that I could not

comprehend at the time, until through testing I found out differently. From Kindergarten to third grade, we lived with site words on his bedroom wall, made tactile letters for the alphabet, jumped on the bed for spelling word practice, reading every day (to, with, and from him), listened to books on car rides, and even canceled tv to stop distractions. I felt that I was so greatly committed to his reading success that I became obsessed and unrelenting.

By the time he finished third grade, I just didn't know how to keep it up anymore. I thought it was ADD at the time and went to my son's pediatrician, conceding defeat as a mother and teacher and just wanting help. It didn't go the way I thought it would. I thought I would get a form, fill it out, give one to his teacher, and be done. Nope.

Fourth grade for him was the "year of doctors" as we called it, followed by the "year of medicines." At the final meeting with the specialist who had started it all, I was overwhelmed into a stupor. He was diagnosed with Pervasive Developmental Disorder Not Otherwise Specified (PDD-NOS), along with other things like dyslexia sprinkled in. I heard words like Autism Spectrum and silent mutism which terrified me. When I got home,

I broke down. My child was "broken" and as a mother I hadn't known. I still tear when I speak of it. Enormous guilt waved over me, for all those years I pushed thinking he wasn't trying hard enough, when in reality, he was trying his hardest. I just didn't know how to reach him best. How could I have? I had no idea what he needed without the testing and diagnosis.

I thought his life was doomed and felt like I had failed him, giving him an enormous hurdle in life that was so unfair. When I finally came to terms with what the diagnoses meant and how I felt about it, I knew I had to act. He needed me to help so I became his advocate. That's what a diagnosis does, it empowers you to help your child succeed the way they need it, not the way parents and teachers often guess that they need it.

Having this experience forever changed the way I saw the world of education and how I felt about those students who truly struggle in heartbreaking ways every day. These struggling students are trapped in a world that doesn't understand them until someone takes the time to dig down beneath the surface, find out the problem, and give them real help. The kind of help that lifts them up and puts them on the path to independence and success for the rest of their life.

Fast forward- he is 22 and doing well. He graduated high school and technical college on time and lives with his dog, Lawrence, in Colorado. He loves to read every day, books I don't even understand. He is a success story.

READING FLUENCY MILESTONES

Kindergarten

___Letter recognition upper and lowercase

___Letter sounds

___K Dolch Site word recognition

First Grade

___*10 words per minute by August

___*30 words per minute by January

___*60 words per minute by June

___CVC (cat) words

___CVCE (late) words

___Digraphs (sh, wh, ch,, th, tch)

___Consonant Blends (tr, sp, br, etc.)

___Compound words

___-ing endings

___-ed endings

___-s endings

___1st Grade Dolch Site word recognition

*words per minute=how many words correct read per minute using a running record assessment

Second Grade

___*60 words per minute in August

___*80 words per minute by January

___*100 words per minute by June

___Vowel digraphs (ea, ee, ai, oo, ou, ie, igh, ay, oy)

___Multisyllabic words (ex. example)

___Prefixes

___suffixes

*words per minute=how many words correct read per minute using a running record assessment

WHAT TO DO IF YOUR CHILD DOESN'T REACH A READING MILESTONE

Listen to your child's teacher for recommendations. You have a very short window of time to keep your child on track. If the recommendation is to test for a disability, the earlier it's diagnosed, the higher the chances of getting back on track in time. It reduces stress between you and your child and your child in the classroom. Your child will then receive the support they need inside and outside the classroom. Private testing is faster and easier than going through the school system. If cost and insurance are an issue, then advocate for your child through your local public school system quickly. It can take up to six months to start testing. An entire school year can go by without any clear information and the right support. However, no official disability diagnosis will be made through school testing; only a doctor can do that.

TIPS TO IMPROVE READING FLUENCY

The best way to increase your child's reading fluency (how fluid your child is reading without having to sound out the words) is to read. Have your child read for 20 minutes a day. This can be done in a combination of ways for different reasons. When done together, it makes the biggest impact. Here's a list to get you going:

1. Practice site words daily
2. Practice weekly spelling patterns
3. Have your child read out loud
4. Have your child read at their independent level
5. Have your child listen to audiobooks above their reading level (ex. in the car)
6. Have your child listen and follow audio books online above their reading level (at home or traveling, try Epic!)
7. Read books with your child above their reading level

So why are there differences between independent and above reading level recommendations? Independent means that your child can easily read the book out loud without sounding out words and understand it. They can read this on their own. This is for enjoyment. If your child's teacher is sending home weekly books to read during the week, it may start off a little bumpy but then get easier the more they read them. Keep reading it. Even when your child says that they've read it already and it's easy for them. It's supposed to be. The more your child sees and reads a word it moves from short term memory to long term memory building their site word knowledge and improving their fluency. You want this.

Read above your child's independent reading level by 1 to improve fluency in a different way. This allows your child to listen to how words they cannot read sound and hear the intonation and cadence of reading aloud. It also exposes your child to higher levels in vocabulary, sentence structure, plot, and characters. It means the book they cannot read by themselves, and feel is out of their reach, they can still have. Stop and discuss what is happening in the story. Make predictions and connect the story to their lives. This is a great opportunity to build on comprehension skills as well as fluency. Have fun with it!

HOW DO I KNOW IF A BOOK IS ON LEVEL FOR MY CHILD?

When out and about or sitting at home, it's good to know if the book your child wants to read is a good fit for them. For quiet reading for enjoyment, you want your child reading at their independent level, not frustration level. There are two easy ways to find out. You can look it up or do a hand count method.

Accelerated Reader Book Finder is a site by Renaissance that uses a quick book look up system by title to tell you the reading level of a book. Go to this site https://www.arbookfind.com and choose parent. Stay in quick search and type in the book title. It will give you a bunch of information. What you're interested in is the book level. To understand this leveling, the number before the decimal is the grade level and the number after the decimal is the month in that grade. So, 2.4 is second grade fourth month. Your child should be able to read this book in November in second grade.

Have your child read a random page of a book (never read before). Use the hand count method. For every word your child doesn't know or reads incorrectly, count one finger. When your hand is fully open (5) the book is at your child's frustration level and should not read by themselves. They will only get frustrated and/or will not understand it. This is a good book to read together. Maybe have them read the first sentence of every paragraph and you read the rest.

HOW TO SUPPORT YOUR CHILD ONLINE

If your child is taking classes online or is in a virtual classroom, it's important to understand that the learning style will be different, and they will need more support from you than if they were in a traditional face-to-face classroom. The best ways to see them succeed will be to follow these guidelines.

Familiarize yourself with the online platform. That is the place where you can find your child's access to their classes. Ask your teacher for a tour if possible. Spend time here clicking on everything. Know how to log in, access lessons, and submit assignments. Find the link for live lessons and test it. Check out where the resources are located and how to connect to them with passwords. Make shortcuts on your child's computer for all resources and log into them. Have the computer remember your child's passwords for quicker access. Then, print the passwords and keep them in a handy place for your child just in case. Finally, make sure your child has the software needed and everything is updated.

Check the learning platform daily. Have print-outs ready the night before so that you know what is being learned and how. The platform will show any assignments and tests due for the week. Keep on top of it. This will ensure that you and your child do not get overwhelmed and will reduce any anxiety.

Set a routine for your child for lesson times, work times, and breaks. Have the school day schedule posted and set alarms for live lessons. Take breaks between screen time. Get up and move between classes to get blood flow and oxygen to the brain. Make sure your child has a space that is distraction free, but that you can check in on them to make sure they are on task. Get a reliable headphone set for them to use so that the class does not hear your background if possible.

Communicate with your child's teacher consistently. Set up a schedule for check-ins. If your child is completely online, once a week or bi-weekly is good. It's a good idea to keep a communication journal to write down any questions and concerns you may have along with any information the teacher gives you.

Support your child by allowing them to struggle, not to tears, but enough for them to be pushed to the next level of learning. Learning is not always easy and sometimes you have to really work at it. We all know this, yet as a parent it's tempting to want to give them the answers to make your life at home smoother, but I promise you that it's not worth it.

Small doses of struggle are normal and good. Use alpha waves music quietly in the background to help stay focused and concentrate. This uses a middle range spectrum in brain wave frequency (8 -12 Hz) in its rhythm to keep the mental state calm and relaxed. You should not even notice the music playing. This one is a personal favorite: https://youtu.be/ GEgSBuYlSoA. When the struggle is too much, take a break, walk away, and talk about it. Maybe extend and enrich the content with a fun activity to connect with and bring it to life. If the struggle continues, contact your teacher, for more support.

CONCLUSION

For maximum student success, parents need to have control in their child's education to best support their child. Whether it's face-to-face, concurrent, or virtual, knowing what your child needs can be the difference between success and failure. When parents partner with teachers the best of both worlds happens, so be involved and be the difference.

Chapter 8:

LEAD TO SHAPE AND INSPIRE

Never doubt that a small group of thoughtful, committed citizens can change the world. Indeed, it's the only thing that ever has.

Margaret Mead

Ideally, all students will read proficiently in third grade regardless of race, ethnicity, ELL status, ESE status, socioeconomic factors, and technology access. All students will be supported and reach their maximum potential both in and out of school for a future that supports them and their future families. So how do we get there? Follow the path laid out in four steps. All three spokes, the education decision makers, teachers, and parents, in the child-centered wheel need to be fully engaged.

First, join a coalition in education to get active and help spread awareness. Everyone in the community needs to know about the full impact not reading on grade level in third grade has on our children. Forty-four percent of children not reading on level in third grade is unacceptable. Raising reading fluency by third grade directly impacts a person's ability to be economically self-sufficient. Children deserve a bright future, not a jail cell.

Next, support easier and faster testing when students are not meeting reading milestones through progress monitoring, beginning in kindergarten. A child's time is too valuable to wait for response to intervention paperwork and meetings that drag out and waste valuable learning time. Children are not expendable. Their future depends on it.

Then, advocate for ELA virtual education in your school system as a viable option to increase reading proficiency and create equity among demographic groups because *it has proven to be effective*. If you had a choice of sending your child to the school across the street or a few blocks over and one had better reading success outcomes than the other, which would you choose? It's a no-brainer. When it comes to our children, we choose the one with the better success rate. Third grade virtual school students scored an average of **eight percentage points higher** than face-to-face third grade students on the State Standards Assessments in English Language Arts between 2015 and 2021. In 2021, it was 18 percentage points!

Finally, push a policy change that changes the way we train teachers. Teachers need to know how to educate the children of the future in classrooms of the future. In order to do that, they need to have an online teaching and learning class focusing on distance education theory and strategies in their methods classes. This change needs to happen through university training for teacher certification and in state recertification for current teachers. Teachers should have the opportunity to have this education at no cost to them, but part of a nationwide catch-up badly needed. They should not have to go to school for a master's degree to have this knowledge.

Figure 28

Four Steps to Make Change

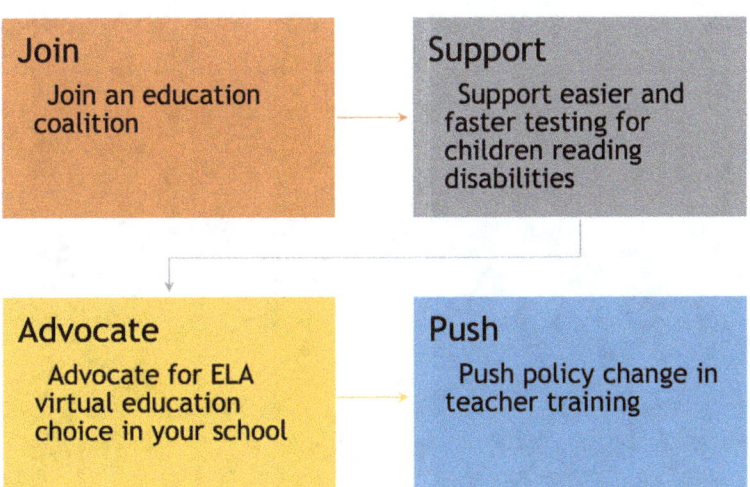

When all three spokes in the child centered wheel are working together, then there will be the change needed in our educational system. The focus needs to always be on the child. If it's not for them, then don't do it. So, get on the track! Become the squeaky wheel and get the grease. Together, let's make change happen!

BIBLIOGRAPHY

- Aljaser, Afaf M. "The Effectiveness of E-Learning Environment in Developing Academic Achievement and the Attitude to Learn English among Primary Students." *Turkish Online Journal of Distance Education* 20, no. 2 (April 25, 2019): 176-94. https://doi.org/10.17718/tojde.557862.

- Brown, Mark, Helen Hughes, Mike Keppell, Natasha Hard, and Liz Smith. "Stories from Students in Their First Semester of Distance Learning." *The International Review of Research in Open and Distributed Learning* 16, no. 4 (November 2, 2015). https://doi.org/10.19173/irrodl.v16i4.1647.

- Burdina, Gulnara M., Irina E. Krapotkina, and Liliya G. Nasyrova. "Distance Learning in Elementary School Classrooms: An Emerging Framework for Contemporary Practice." *International Journal of Instruction* 12, no. 1 (January 3, 2019): 1-16. https://doi.org/10.29333/iji.2019.1211a.

- Chapman, T., D. Dick, P. Ford, P. Henry, K. Hobert, M. Keller, K. Riley, C. Tidwell, and R. Wright. "Increasing Success with Online Degree Courses and Programs in the VCCS." *Inquiry* 22, no. 1 (2019): 1-15.

- Curtis, Heidi, and Loredana Werth. "Fostering Student Success and Engagement in a K-12 Online School." *Journal of Online Learning Research* 1, no. 2 (2015): 163-90. https://files.eric.ed.gov/fulltext/EJ1148836.pdf.

- Fiester, L. "Early Warning Confirmed." *Annie E. Casey Foundation.* 2013. http://gradelevelreading.net/wp-content/uploads/2013/11/EarlyWarningConfirmed.pdf.

- "Early Warning! Why Reading by the End of Third Grade Matters." *Annie E. Casey Foundation*, 2010. https://www.aecf.org/resources/early-warning-why-reading-by-the-end-of-third-grade-matters/.
- Florida TaxWatch. "Final Report: A Comprehensive Assessment of Florida Virtual School." October 31, 2007. https://floridataxwatch.org. https://floridataxwatch.org/Research/Blog/ArtMID/34888/ArticleID/16048/Final-Report-A-Comprehensive-Assessment-of-Florida-Virtual-School.
- Hanover Research. "Critical Academic Indicators." *Hanover Research*. Washington, DC: Hanover Research, June 2014. www.hanoverresearch.com.
- Hernandez, Donald J. "Double Jeopardy: How Third Grade Reading Skills and Poverty Influence High School Graduation." Baltimore, Maryland: The Annie E. Casey Foundation, 2012.
- Huang, Xiaoxia, Aruna Chandra, Concetta A. DePaolo, and Lakisha L. Simmons. "Understanding Transactional Distance in Web-Based Learning Environments: An Empirical Study." *British Journal of Educational Technology* 47, no. 4 (March 16, 2016): 734–47. https://doi.org/10.1111/bjet.12263.
- Huang, Xiaoxia, Aruna Chandra, Concetta DePaolo, Jennifer Cribbs, and Lakisha Simmons. "Measuring Transactional Distance in Web-Based Learning Environments: An Initial Instrument Development." *Open Learning: The Journal of Open, Distance and E-Learning* 30, no. 2 (May 4, 2015): 106–26. https://doi.org/10.1080/02680513.2015.1065720.

- Hughes, John, Chengfu Zhou, and Yaacov Petscher. "Comparing Success Rates for General and Credit Recovery Courses Online and Face to Face: Results for Florida High School Courses." *Regional Educational Laboratory Southeast,* September 2015. https://ies.ed.gov/ncee/edlabs.

- McNally, Susan. "The Effectiveness of Florida Virtual School in Terms of Coast and Student Achievement in a Selected Florida School District." Doctoral dissertation, 2012. https://eric.ed.gov/?id=ED554780.

- McNamara, John K., Mary Scissons, and Naomi Gutknecth. "A Longitudinal Study of Kindergarten Children at Risk for Reading Disabilities." *Journal of Learning Disabilities* 44, no. 5 (July 19, 2011): 421–30. https://doi.org/10.1177/0022219411410040.

- Molnar, Alex, Gary Miron, Najat Elgeberi, Michael K Barbour, Luis Huerta, Sheryl Rankin Shafer, and Jennifer King Rice. "Virtual Schools in the U.S. 2019." National Education Policy Center. NEPC, May 28, 2019. https://nepc.colorado.edu/publication/virtual-schools-annual-2019.

- Moore, Michael. "Theory of Transactional Distance." In *Theoretical Principals of Distance Education,* edited by D. Keegan, 22–38. Routledge, 1997. http://www.c3l.uni-oldenburg.de/cde/found/moore93.pdf.

- NASSP. "NASSP." National Association of Secondary School Principals, 2021. https://www.nassp.org.

- Prescott, Jen Elise, Kristine Bundschuh, Elizabeth R. Kazakoff, and Paul Macaruso. "Elementary School–

Wide Implementation of a Blended Learning Program for Reading Intervention." *The Journal of Educational Research* 111, no. 4 (April 19, 2017): 497–506. https://doi.org/10.1080/00220671.2017.1302914.

- Snow, C., S. Burns, and P. Griffin. "Preventing Reading Difficulties in Young Children." Washington DC: National Academy Press, 1998. https://files.eric.ed.gov/fulltext/ED416465.pdf.
- Spector, J. Michael. Handbook of Research on *Educational Communications and Technology.* New York: Springer, 2014.
- The Community Center for Education Results. "The Road Map Project 2013 Results Report." *The Road Map Project.* Seattle, Washington: The Community Center for Education Results, 2014. https://roadmapproject.org/wp-content/uploads/2018/09/2013-Results-Report_Reduced-File-Sz.pdf.
- Thompson, Virginia L., and Yonghong L. McDowell. "A Case Study Comparing Student Experiences and Success in an Undergraduate Mathematics Course Offered through Online, Blended, and Face-To-Face Instruction." *International Journal of Education in Mathematics Science and Technology* 7, no. 2 (April 11, 2019): 116–36. https://doi.org/10.18404/ijemst.552411.
- Waddell, Sherrill. "Examining the Relationship between Virtual School Size and Student Achievement." *Quarterly Review of Distance Education* 18, no. 4 (2017): 23–35.

Dr. Lisa Richardson Hassler

ABOUT THE AUTHOR

Chicago native author, Dr. Lisa Richardson Hassler, has been in the field of education for two decades with degrees in Elementary Education, Online Teaching and Learning, and Educational Leadership. She is state certified in Elementary Education, Educational Leadership, and English Speakers of Other Languages. Her experience includes teaching first through fourth grades in public, private, and Montessori schools.

Hassler was the recipient of the National Louis University 2022 Outstanding Dissertation Award in the category of Advancing Professional Practice. Reviewers commented on the many strengths of her dissertation, particularly her data analysis and the usability and strength of her recommendations. In 2019, she was nominated for the Golden Halo Award by her students and parents for being an inspiring Christian teacher. Her previous work includes Family Second Language Acquisition and An Evaluation of Virtual School's Preparation of Second Grade Student's for Third Grade Reading Proficiency.

Lisa is currently a second-grade teacher in Florida and enjoys beekeeping with her husband. *America's Embarrassing Reading Crisis: What We Learned From COVID,* is her first book.

drlisarhassler.com
LinkedIn: @drlisarichardsonhassler
Twitter: @drlisarhassler
Facebook: @DrLisaRichardsonHassler
IG: @drlisarichardsonhassler

www.ingramcontent.com/pod-product-compliance
Lightning Source LLC
Chambersburg PA
CBHW071156120626
46546CB00006B/2294